Drawing for interior designers

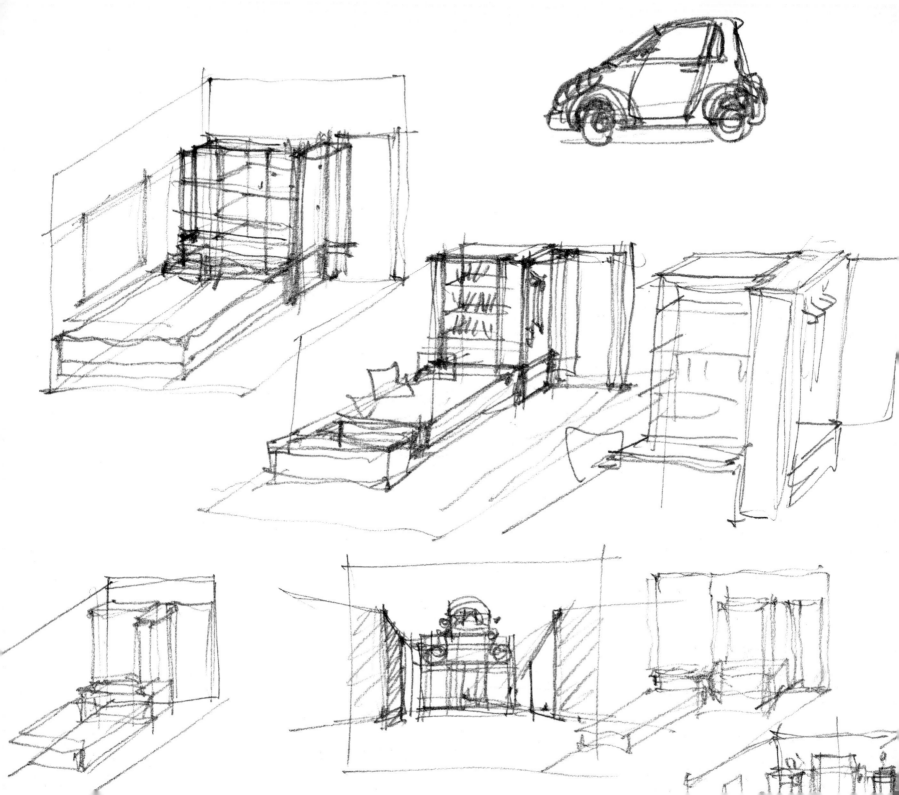

Gilles Ronin

Drawing for interior designers

Bloomsbury Visual Arts
An imprint of Bloomsbury Publishing Plc

B L O O M S B U R Y
LONDON · OXFORD · NEW YORK · NEW DELHI · SYDNEY

Bloomsbury Visual Arts
An imprint of Bloomsbury Publishing Plc

Imprint previously known as A&C Black Visual Arts

50 Bedford Square   1385 Broadway
London   New York
WC1B 3DP   NY 10018
UK   USA

www.bloomsbury.com

First published in Great Britain in 2010
by A&C Black Publishers
Reprinted by Bloomsbury Visual Arts in 2014, 2016 and 2017

British Library Cataloguing-in-Publication Data
A catalogue record for this book is available from the British Library.

ISBN: 978-1-4081-2991-3

Page design: Florence Le Maux
Cover design: James Watson
Photography: Olivier Ploton
English text layout: Penny Mills
Translator: Alexa Stace

Printed and bound in India

To find out more about our authors and books visit www.bloomsbury.com. Here you will find extracts,
author interviews, details of forthcoming events and the option to sign up for our newsletters.

contents

Introduction

Sitting quietly at home, sketchbook in hand, is the ideal way to tackle drawing. In fact, your home is an absolute mine of subjects to draw. Perhaps you already have a plan in your head for a makeover or conversion?

House space not only contains objects to be drawn, but offers a setting, enabling you to understand perspective and to explore the different ways of depicting space. Once you have grasped the principles, drawing will become a game, even a pleasure.

If you want to study a little carpentry project, take down a partition wall, or simply dream about what you could do later, you will find here how to draw a layout, enabling you to make several plans for your space. It's also a good exercise in drawing.

You will also find here the practical principles which will help you put your plans down on paper and better express your ideas, for no serious project gets made without a progressive plan.

It is also an opportunity to learn some tricks of the trade and conventions which are part of an architect's know-how and which will help with ideas.

The relationship between a drawing and a project is at the heart of this book, and is reciprocal. If the capacity to represent a space is the prerequisite for converting it, and is a technique to be acquired, the different variations also offer many absorbing exercises for those learning to draw.

Representing an interior space

You don't need to make a drawing to take out a partition wall. But if the situation is more complicated, you cannot think it through without some support. By putting your ideas down on paper they can then develop and enlarge, not just as disconnected thoughts and ideas, but coherently. A freehand drawing in pencil gives you the liberty to be creative.

Developing your project

It is by means of several kinds of representation, drawings and plans, that we learn how to develop a project. In this book, some of these representations are based on real spaces – houses and flats – and we will give you finished examples of real conversions, like the numerous books on home decoration or interior design which you will find in the public library. But because you live in your own space, the examples you find are never just right. This book therefore aims to show above all a real method of drawing, with a progressive acquisition of the skills which will enable you to carry out operations logically, and to put your own ideas down on paper.

The progression

First of all there are the principal drawings, like the ground plan and the section, the technique of scale drawing, which allows you to measure the spaces to be converted, and then finally the different kinds of perspective which enable you to understand space, while studying its modifications.

Variations and transformations

From the first you will be confronted with the practice of conversion. Getting into the habit of varying elements from the start, on the graphics side as well as from a model, is way of better understanding the rules of design, at the same time as inventing modifications, of finding and projecting ideas.

Let's take an example. You can draw a particular space or room like a camera, strictly copying what is in front of you, but you would not be making use of the rules which permit you to show the space in question a little differently: a partition less, some panels here and a transparent space there, the ceiling taken down to increase the loft space, and why not a flight of stairs to facilitate access, etc.

Some of the elementary principles of perspective and some professional tricks will teach you to think intelligently about your drawing, as though it were a little mechanism where you can move the parts about.

From the first pages on line, its values and colours, we get into the habit of grafting on variations and new creations.

Themes such as a small conversion (of a bedroom, sitting-room or kitchen) will be introduced progressively, but also more general, architectural ideas, such as depth, thickness, geometry and transparency.

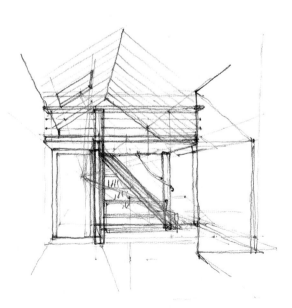

PREPARATION FOR DRAWING

Learn and practise basic freehand drawing techniques. These are indispensable for all representational drawing, and you will need some understanding of these skills for the following chapters.

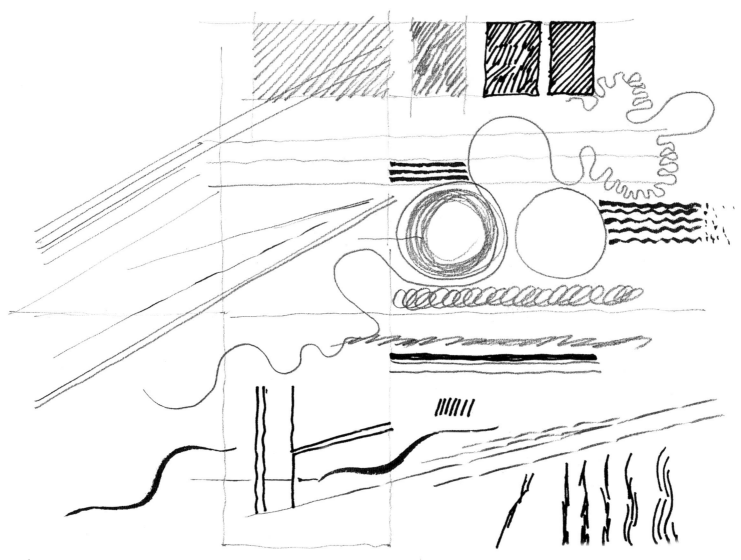

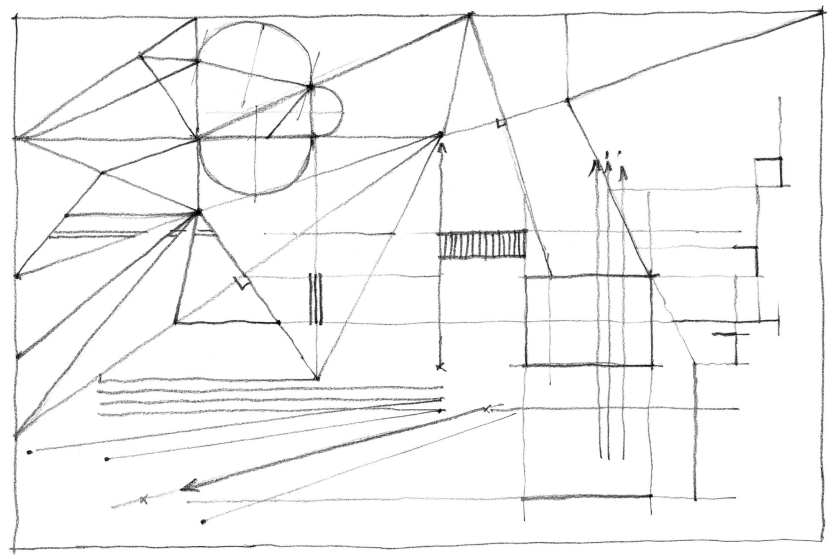

Materials

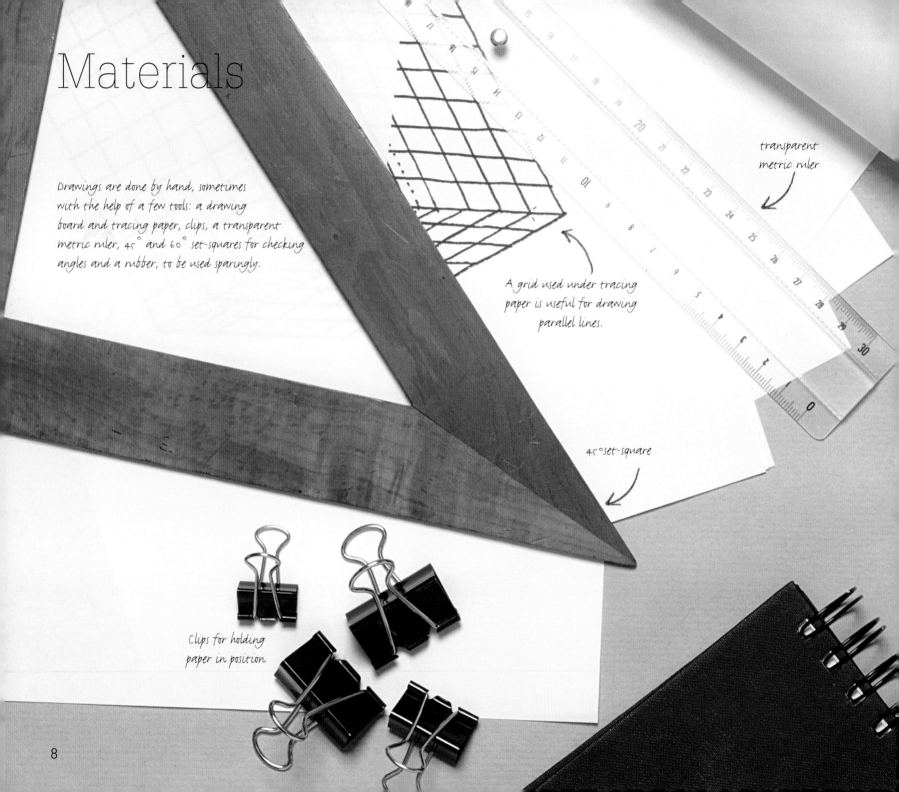

Drawings are done by hand, sometimes with the help of a few tools: a drawing board and tracing paper, clips, a transparent metric ruler, 45° and 60° set-squares for checking angles and a rubber, to be used sparingly.

transparent metric ruler

A grid used under tracing paper is useful for drawing parallel lines.

45° set-square

Clips for holding paper in position

The Paper

The paper used depends on whether it is a single drawing, or a succession of drawings as part of a study. In the first case, a sketchbook with a stiff cover is indispensable if you are moving about. If you are going to tint the drawing with watercolours, use 300 gm paper, preferably in a block, to avoid the problem of crinkling.

If you are making a progressive study, you will need to superimpose drawings over the initial layout. The ideal paper is slightly transparent – 50-60gsm is ideal, but becoming difficult to find. Tracing paper, either in a roll or in leaves, replaces it but has a rougher surface for the pencil.

Black felt-tip

propelling pencil, 0.5 or 0.7mm HB, allows many modulations of line, and is useful for inevitable small corrections. It is the simplest and lightest pencil, allowing you to have the most direct connection possible between hand, paper and thought.

Cut your rubber into small pieces to make it easier to handle, or use a rubber made from soft bread, which is softer and easier on the paper.

A tape measure is indispensable.

The line

Drawing a line is a reflection of your attitude and your personality. The kind of line – direct, clean, clumsy, hesitant, heavy, light, incisive etc – depends on your personality. It improves with practice, as you will see with these few warming-up exercises.

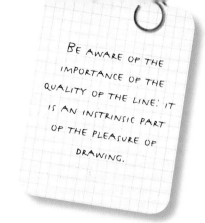

BE AWARE OF THE IMPORTANCE OF THE QUALITY OF THE LINE: IT IS AN INTRINSIC PART OF THE PLEASURE OF DRAWING.

Draw some straight lines from one point to another, without looking at the tip of the pencil too much. Just skim over the paper the first time, as if to register the distance, then draw it the second time.

The line

A line is not just a thing in itself. It represents something – it is a symbol of a contour, an axis, a horizon, the motifs on the floor or the setting of the door-frame. A line has a form, most often straight, a point of departure and arrival, a position in space and on the page, an orientation. In practical terms a line is the route between two points, and it is the points that are critical and must be well placed.

Graphics, tonal values and colours

You have to show surfaces, shadows, differences of tone in your drawing. But the pencil is not made for showing a surface. Work out a range of values, in small 2–3cm squares, from the lightest to the darkest, in five or six stages, then do gradations. Note how you can avoid it looking too mechanical by combining repetition and variations.

Fill the spaces, creating 'greys' with hatching, dots, small regular lines, etc. Vary the intensity, without clogging up the surface too much.

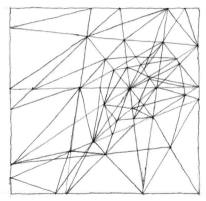

This drawing is made up of lines, added progressively from points made at random, then joined up freehand. This creates other intersections which can be joined up in their turn, and so on.

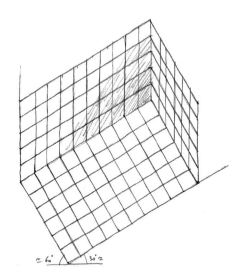

Draw some horizontal lines, and vertical ones, because they present a particular difficulty, while being the most usual ones in architectural drawing. This exercise can be done by drawing a network of parallel lines, then making a grid of perpendicular lines.

Figures

The construction of certain shapes, notably the square, and then the circle, is a permanent exercise in drawing. The shapes enable us to see the value of the vertical and horizontal, basis of all proportion and orientation of line, in brief the measure of the whole drawing. The constructions are limbering-up exercises, to practise regularly, like going to the gym!

Draw a circle inside a square by drawing the diagonals and the median points of the triangles, as in this series.

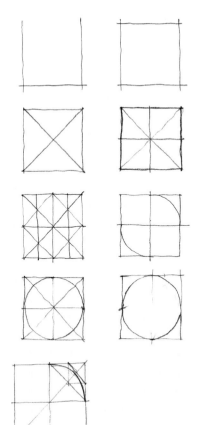

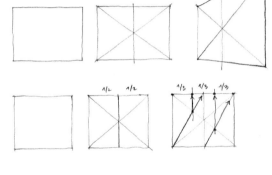

In the square, draw the diagonals, which then give you the mid-point of the sides and the median point of the square. This operation has a purpose – later on it enables you to draw shapes in perspective and in space, to divide a segment into several parts and to recognise the main angles – 45°, 30° and 60°).

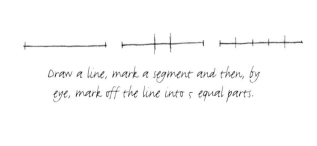

Draw a line, mark a segment and then, by eye, mark off the line into 5 equal parts.

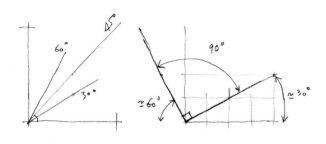

At the base of a square practise drawing angles of 30°, 45°, 60° and 90°.

Proportions

Proportions are relative measurements. We are not discussing aesthetics here, it is simply a question of the length of connection between the various elements and the distance between the various points in the drawing. Note that, if you get these connections absolutely right at all points, your drawing will be perfectly accurate. This is a vital skill to master.

When drawing, get into the habit of observing proportions, and watch out for the errors which will inevitably arise. To look at the proportions of a rectangle, the simplest way is to compare it mentally with one or several squares.

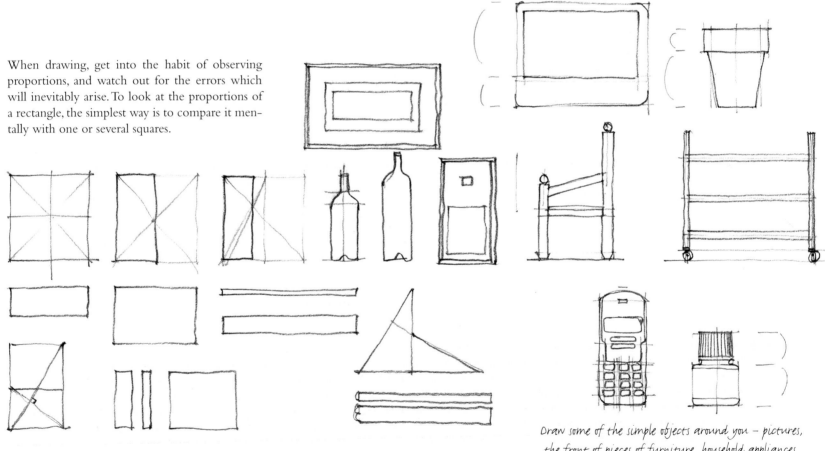

Draw some rectangles, starting with squares which you then divide up.

Draw some of the simple objects around you – pictures, the front of pieces of furniture, household appliances, small utensils. Pay careful attention to their proportions, which give each object its own visual identity and indicate their function.

Constructing a drawing

For your first try, choose a wall panel, with a door, window, picture frames, pieces of furniture etc. Draw it all on the flat, as though there were no perspective (there probably is) respecting not just the proportions of each element, but showing how they align, the diagonal, horizontal and vertical lines which connect all these objects. This operation is what we call constructing the drawing.

Practise drawing horizontal and vertical lines.

Then practise drawing the elements of a section of wall. Take the opportunity to visualise what it would look like if you changed round some of these elements.

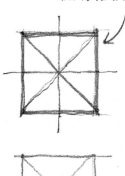
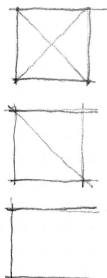

13

PLANS AND LAYOUTS

To draw a plan of a certain space, you should in theory have made a note of all the dimensions beforehand. The plan and the layout to scale are thus closely related. But, to make this layout, you have to understand the principal rules of representation, then you will see better how to organise your work. This is why we are going to start by showing the principles behind the plan.

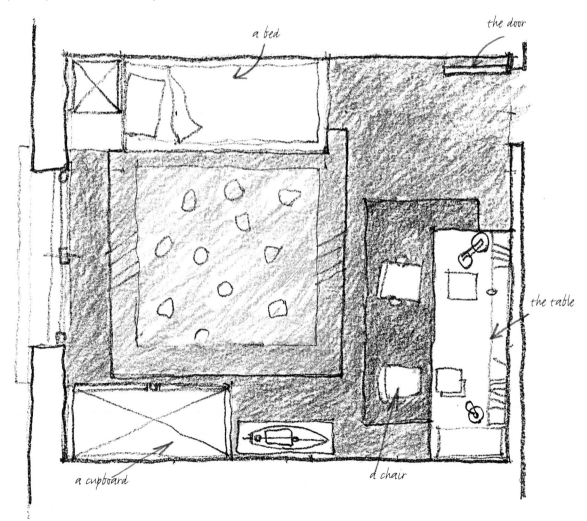

a bed

the door

the table

a cupboard

a chair

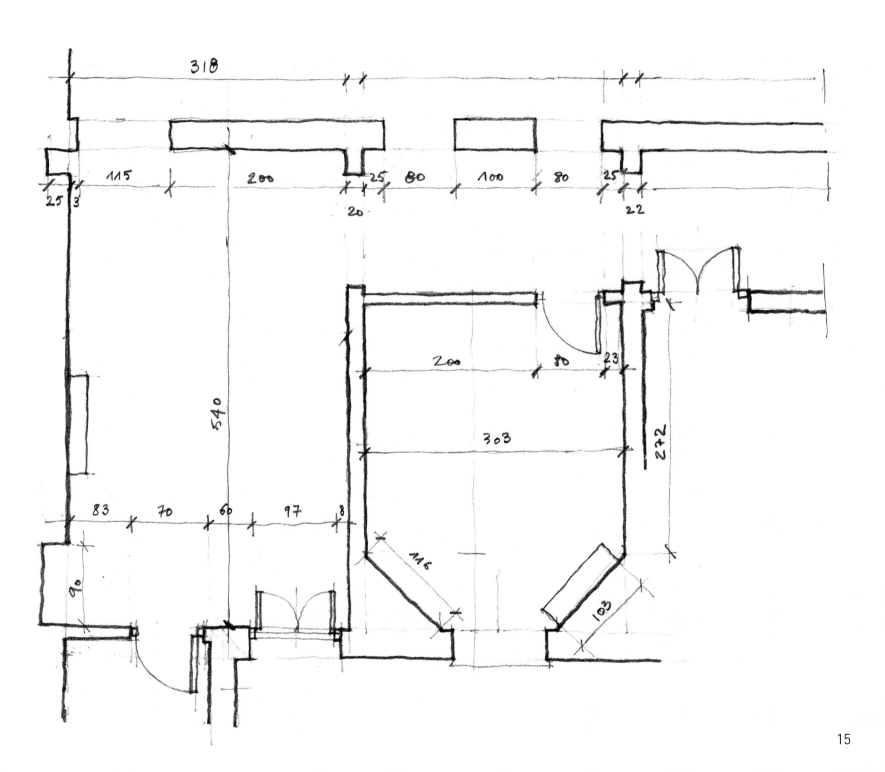

318

115   200   25   80   100   80   25

25   3   20   22

540

200   80   23

303   272

83   70   60   97   8

90   116

103

15

Drawing the plan

The plan or layout is a view from above. An elevation, (horizontal view, face on, if you like) works on the same principle, with a scale, to which you add some codes and conventions that save time and make the plan easier to read.

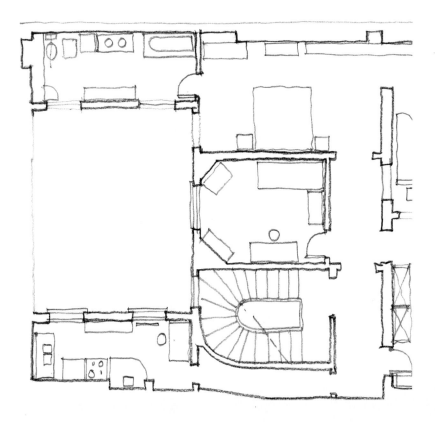

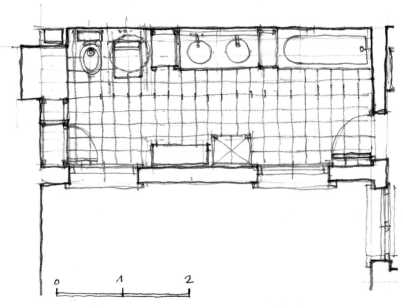

1/50 or 2cm per m

1/100 or 1cm per m

Here are three plans of the same flat, with three different scales. We have not shown exactly the same view of the space, or the same objects in detail.

Scales

The scale is the connection in size between the drawing and reality. Scale allows us to measure distances on a plan or a map.

Note that there is no scale on a sketch or in a perspective drawing, since the objects, varying in size according to the distance, are not measurable.

Each object is drawn to scale

Scale is expressed by a fraction, such as 1/10, called a tenth. For the interior of a house or flat the scale of 1/50 is currently used. This can also be expressed as 2cm to the metre, or 2cm p.m. (There are 50 times 2cm in a metre.)

At this scale a room measuring 4 x 6m becomes, on paper, a rectangle of 8 x 12cm. You can show rooms, staircases, kitchen equipment etc. in the space, but to give details you need a 'larger' scale, such as 1/20 or 1/10.

Making a graphic scale

If you don't like doing mental calculations, draw a little scale on the plan. In this way you can measure, and even just take in at a glance, the dimensions of the spaces and objects represented.

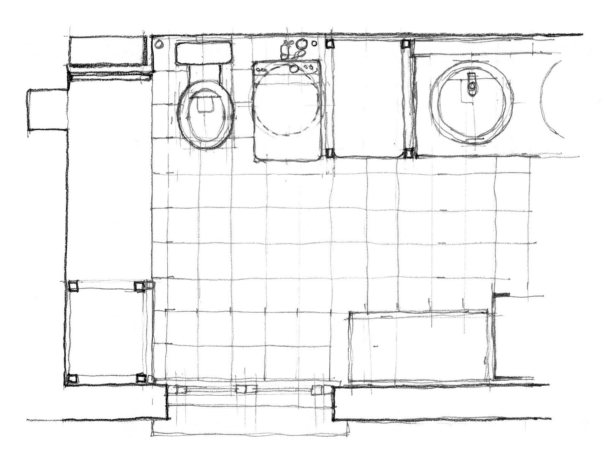

0,2   0.5   1

1/20 or 5cm per m

THE 1 IS ALWAYS THE ORIGINAL. THE FIGURE UNDERNEATH TELLS HOW MANY TIMES THE ORIGINAL HAS BEEN DIVIDED FOR THE DRAWING.

17

Conventions and symbols

Conventions are an interesting aspect of plan drawings. As it is not possible to give the details of some elements which are either too small, or otherwise too repetitive, such as doors, windows etc, we use symbols.

Doors

Doors are shown open, their width to scale, indicating if they open inwards or outwards. You don't draw a line for the threshold. Avoid showing the door with a diagonal line – on the contrary take the chance to practise drawing a quarter-circle! The symbol is simple, showing just the frame and the top of the door (thickness may or may not be shown to scale). Only the passage through is really shown to scale.

Windows

Windows (except for French windows) are shown by two perpendicular lines on the wall, showing the width of the ledge. They are usually shown shut (see p16).

Conventions regarding lines

Unlike a sketch, in a scale drawing the thickness of the lines must be consistent and regular, because they signify something. When drawing in ink, or with instruments, the thickness is strictly controlled, but when using pencil you are in control. It's a good exercise!

A base line, or contour

It shows an edge in the space, an outline, for example the top of a piece of furniture or the banister of a staircase. In fact you don't make many lines of this kind on a plan drawing.

A thin line

This shows details which are not structural – strips of parquet, motifs on a wall, elements in low relief etc.

Thin dotted line

This shows the outline of large elements which are above the plan, such as a large beam, or the boundaries of a mezzanine or overhang.

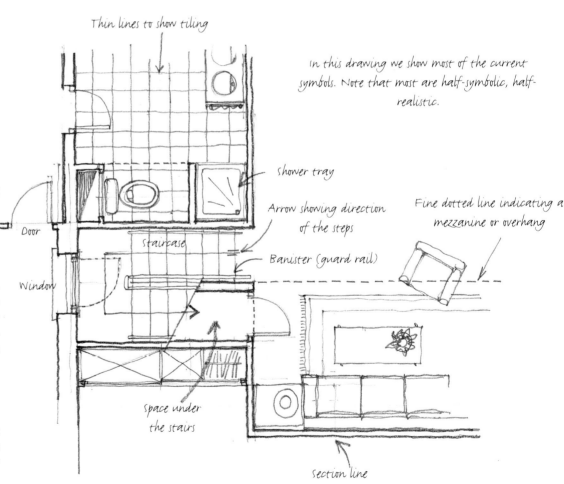

Thin lines to show tiling

In this drawing we show most of the current symbols. Note that most are half-symbolic, half-realistic.

shower tray

Arrow showing direction of the steps

Fine dotted line indicating a mezzanine or overhang

Door

Staircase

Banister (guard rail)

Window

space under the stairs

Section line

Lines indicating dimensions
See p24

The section line and the walls
When you make a floor plan, in principle you show everything under a certain height. By convention, this is fixed at 1 metre from the ground. Everything above this height is left out of the plan. But there are certain elements which come up from the ground and go higher than this fixed height, e.g. the outside walls and partition walls. On a floor plan these are shown cut off, as if a horizontal blade had separated them from the upper part. The passage of this blade defines the section. To differentiate the section it is drawn with a very heavy line.

The stairs
You also show what is under the stairs, as for example a small storage space. The banister, or guard rail, is shown by two lines. To indicate the direction of the stairs draw an arrow, always indicating upstairs.

The logic behind the symbols
Note that there is always a logic in these conventions: a single line indicates an outline, two lines two outlines, which here makes the top of the banister, or handrail. When the section line arrives at the windows, it is replaced by two thin little lines, closed-up, which indicate the thickness of the glass.

Showing furniture and equipment
In general, pieces of furniture are not shown on a ground plan, since they are not permanent. But if their presence is useful on your layout, you can choose to show them exactly, or to use symbols, as shown below.

Fixed sanitary ware is always shown (these are not furniture). Kitchen furniture is variable, and you can decide for yourself.

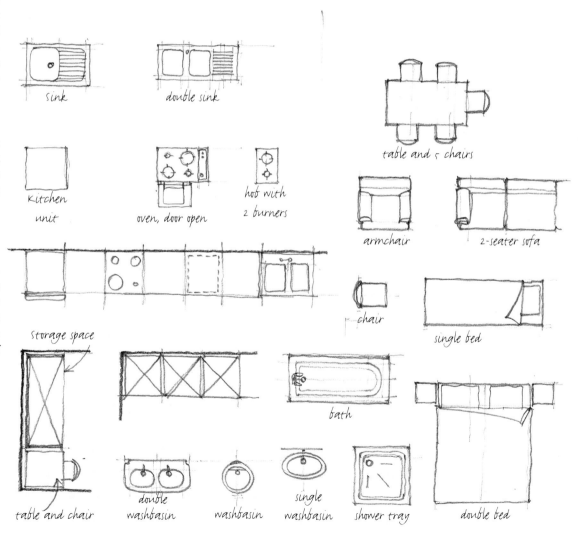

sink

double sink

Kitchen unit

oven, door open

hob with 2 burners

storage space

table and chair

double washbasin

washbasin

single washbasin

shower tray

table and 5 chairs

armchair

2-seater sofa

chair

single bed

bath

double bed

Changing around the furniture

Get used to working on a floor plan, laying out the different arrangements of furniture you could have in the same room. Draw a plan of the room you are in now, then change the furniture around. This exercise will get you accustomed to understanding the dimensions of various elements, being aware of their proportions and thinking about the empty spaces which enable people to move about a room.

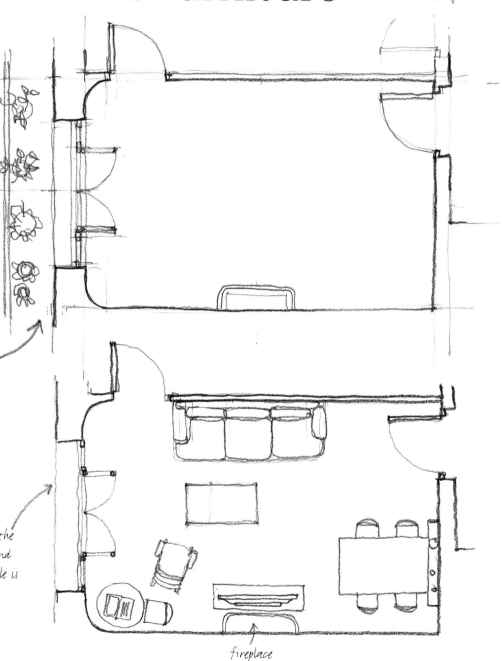

First make a plan of the room without furniture. You can photocopy this as many times as necessary.

First arrangement: the sofa is opposite the fireplace, which has been boarded up and hidden by the television. The dining table is rather close to the kitchen door.

fireplace

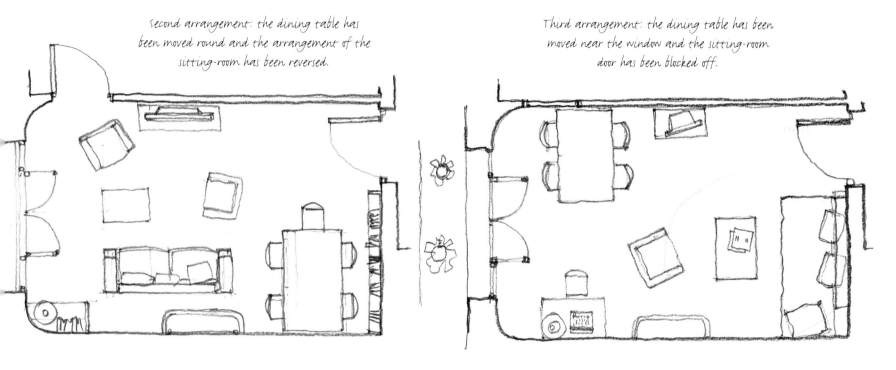

Second arrangement: the dining table has been moved round and the arrangement of the sitting-room has been reversed.

Third arrangement: the dining table has been moved near the window and the sitting-room door has been blocked off.

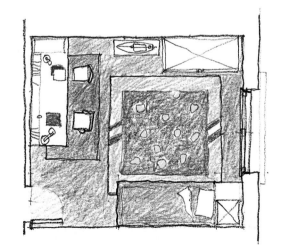

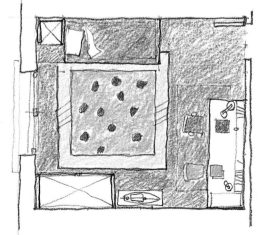

TO HELP PLAN A FURNITURE REARRANGEMENT, YOU CAN COLOUR YOUR DRAWING AND CONSIDER HOW THE ROOM WILL WORK BEFORE MAKING ANY NEW PURCHASES.

Elevation and section

An elevation is a straight-on view of a wall. If you stand back, looking at the wall horizontally, you have a full-face view of the wall, known as an elevation. The principle is the same as for the floor plan. The side walls are thus sectioned vertically, as they were horizontally on the floor plan. This elevation can be called a sectional elevation.

The drawing is of what is facing you, the items against the wall: doors and windows, but also shelves and tables, making an ensemble, like a small façade in your room. Side passages, doors and windows are always cut off, but avoid cutting a single isolated item, such as a column. All this is important: the line of section must indicate the volume in general and the openings, even if they are not exactly opposite.

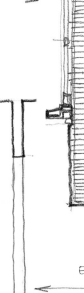

Section of a bathroom, to the scale 1/20, which is more suitable for drawing small spaces and the arrangement of details such as cupboards, bookcases. Note the thickness of the section line, to help differentiate the empty space.

Elevation of a sitting-room, with a small balcony on the left, and to the right a doorway. Scale 1/50.

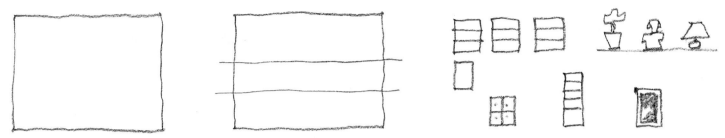

Draw your room in elevation (face-on)

Draw the various items to be included

Rearranging an area of wall

Rethinking the layout of a flat doesn't always mean moving interior walls. Rearranging a wall panel, changing the decoration and objects displayed is in itself an important modification. You can plan this on paper, especially if you are thinking of buying new elements such as shelves, storage boxes, sets of drawers etc.

Design in modules

Take measurements of the various elements to be included, and imagine the various different ways they could be put together. They will be much more interesting if you have worked them out in a drawing: they then become real little compositions, combining practicality with aesthetics.

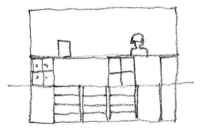

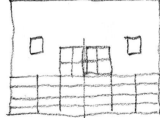

Making a layout

The layout consists of producing a ground plan and elevations of a building, or one of its parts, after taking measurements on the spot. There are thus two phases: taking measurements and copying them out on the documents.

Organisation of the layout

We start with preliminary drawings on which we mark the measurements taken. These drawings are an intermediate stage between the sketch and the ground plan: they are done by hand, on the spot, but with most of the codes in place. Now that you are (more or less) fully informed on all the ways of showing what you can see, you must get ready to take the measurements.

A team effort

Ideally there should be three people involved: one to draw and take notes, and two to hold the tape when large areas are involved. At home, you can get your family involved in this operation. But if you are on your own you'll just have to manage.

A sketch of the ground plan

This is the moment to apply the principles of drawing laid out on page 10. Start by making a freehand plan in a hardback notebook, preferably room by room. Leave space around the drawing for writing down the measurements. At this stage the exact scale of the drawing doesn't matter because you are going to mark it in. Try to keep the drawing in proportion, so that it is easier to read.

The dimensions

These are indicated on a parallel line in the same direction, with small lines to indicate where the measurement runs, and little bias marks to indicate that it's a measurement, not part of the drawing. Be methodical!

Walls and partitions

When marking down the measurements of each room, there is a tendency to forget the thickness of the walls or panels. Take measurement twice, to guard against mistakes. Measure against the real flat surface, not the thick mouldings on the doors or wall panels.

Details

The amount of detail required depends on your final intention. For a flat, don't include panel mouldings. But if you are planning to reorganise a library, or similar, you probably should include them.

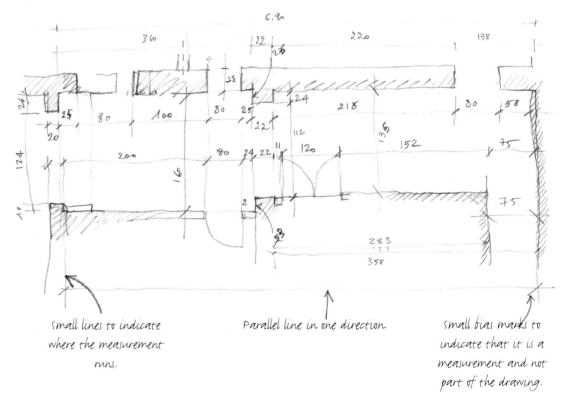

small lines to indicate where the measurement runs.

Parallel line in one direction.

small bias marks to indicate that it is a measurement and not part of the drawing.

Tidying up the floor plan/drawing the whole thing

You can now go on to a drawing of the whole thing. Think of the floor plan as a good sketch which you want to improve or tidy up. Of course you can work in two stages: a first sketch as a foundation, and then superimpose a final drawing.

Format and scale

Now it's time to choose a scale. Let's think of an example. If you are doing a layout of a flat of 100m², more or less square, it will be around 10m x 10m. At a scale of 1/50 (or 2cm per m.) it will be a square 20cm x 20cm, which could go in an A4 format. But it will be too cramped, as you must always leave some space around the drawing. Thus an A3 format (29.7cm x 42cm) or even larger (50cm x 65cm) would be more appropriate. Of course, you can cram in a little more in a sketchbook.

Constructing the floor plan

You must first of all make an outline, that's to say trace out the lines which will not be visible at the final stage of the work, but which will help to ensure that the visible lines are well positioned.

Study the layout

Before drawing the floor plan, make little sketches of it, diagrams in which you can analyse the general dimensions. Without really making a final plan, it's a way of understanding its logic.

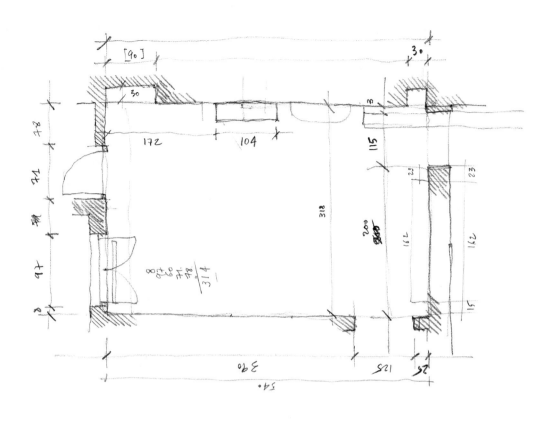

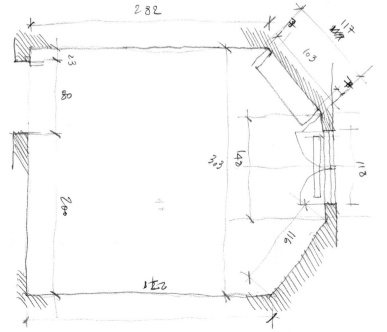

25

Layout of a flat

In this example we go on to the layout of a whole flat. The drawings on these two pages show the different stages, and the progressive fine-tuning of the drawing as we sketch and verify the details.

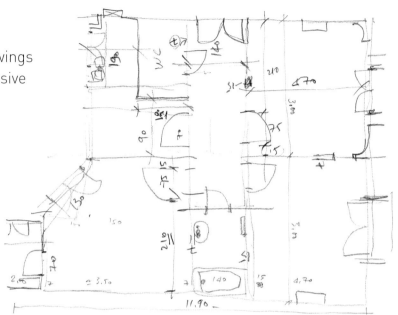

This first layout, made in situ, has been based on the fact that the floor plan of the flat is really simple and can be summed up in a few dimensions.
The drawing is not to scale.

Still at the rough copy stage, this second drawing details the measurements.

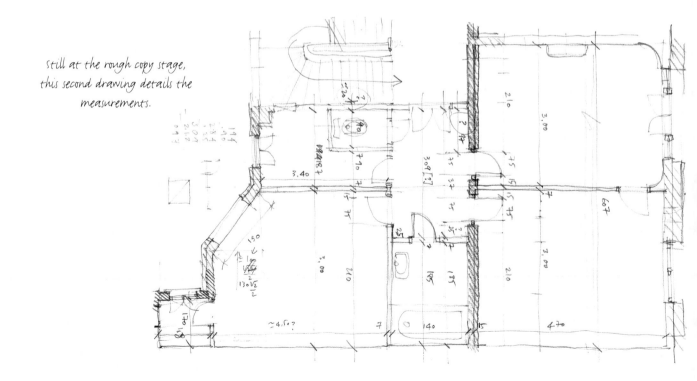

In this third drawing, all the information needed for an interior project is
laid out. See the details of the project on page 38.

PERSPECTIVE

In a scale drawing you have a good view of the location and can take measurements as accurately as you could in the actual space. Moreover, this is the drawing most used in building work.

In order to do this, you need to train yourself to look at space differently from the way you normally perceive it. Thus we are now going to consider more 'visual' methods of representation – the different kinds of perspective.

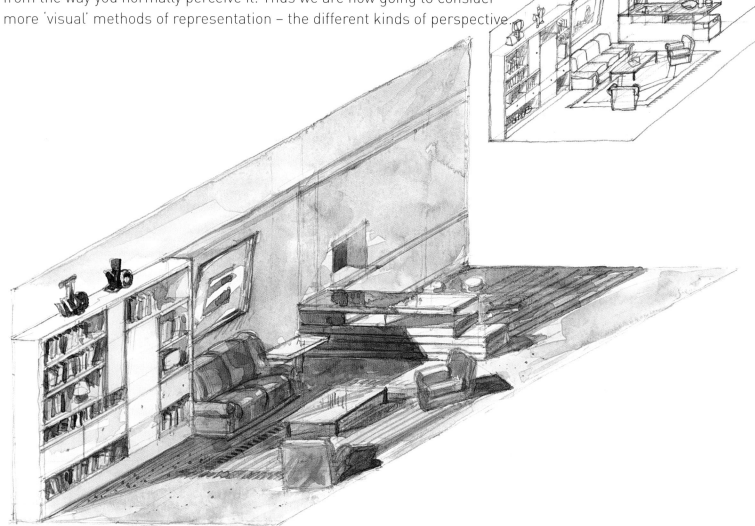

Horizon

29

Isometric projection

This form of perspective is very easy to apply. Moreover it enables you eventually to take measurements, as with a floor plan. In effect, the parallel lines do not converge towards the vanishing point; they stay parallel. Several variations exist, according to the angle of sight chosen: nearer to the layout, or nearer to the elevation.

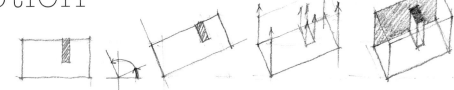

The simplest way to tackle this notion is to arrange a layout on a bias, inclined in front of you and lightly pivoted. Note that you just need to draw some vertical lines (parallel to the sides of the paper) to find the walls.
Note also that when you incline and turn the layout, the rectangles of the faces of the walls take on the aspect of a parallelogram. The opposing sides stay parallel to each other. The view is distorted in relation to the ground plan, but keeps this regularity.

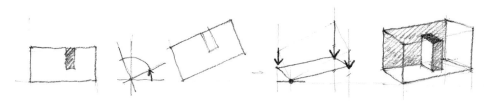

1. We can, when the plan has been pivoted, lower the height of the angles, as the arrows indicate. The view favours the faces of the walls, to the detriment of the geometry of the plan.

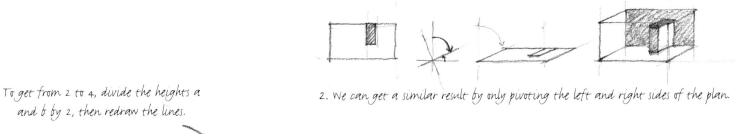

2. We can get a similar result by only pivoting the left and right sides of the plan.

To get from 2 to 4, divide the heights a and b by 2, then redraw the lines.

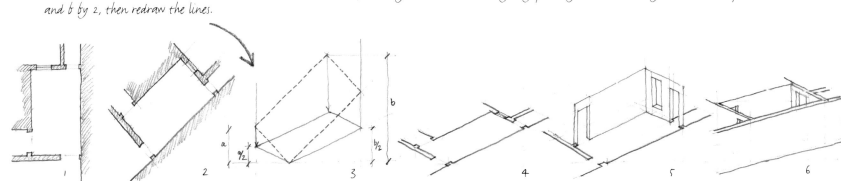

1   2   3   4   5   6

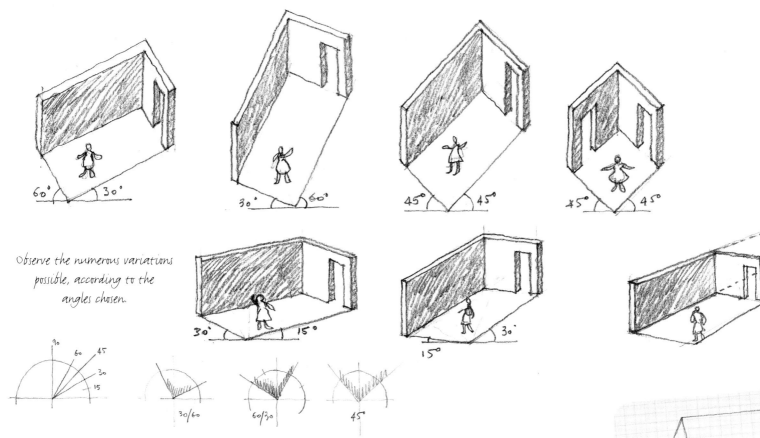

60° 30°　　30° 60°　　45° 45°　　45° 45°

Observe the numerous variations possible, according to the angles chosen.

30° 15°　　15° 30°

90 60 45 30 15

30/60　　60/30　　45°

An effect of reduction

The projection view does not distort length. It produces a paradoxical optical illusion: thinking we are seeing in perspective, we find that the vertical lines, that's to say the walls, are higher than in reality because, if the perspective was true, they would effectively be dwarfed by the effect of distance.

To mitigate this impression we can correct it a little by reducing the height, but then you lose the chance of taking measurements. Note that measurements are only taken while the vertical lines stay parallel, and parallel to the sides of the floor plan.

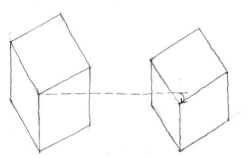

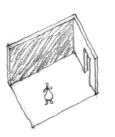

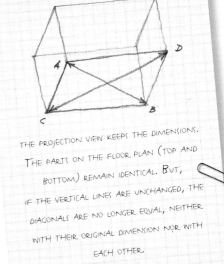

THE PROJECTION VIEW KEEPS THE DIMENSIONS. THE PARTS ON THE FLOOR PLAN (TOP AND BOTTOM) REMAIN IDENTICAL. BUT, IF THE VERTICAL LINES ARE UNCHANGED, THE DIAGONALS ARE NO LONGER EQUAL, NEITHER WITH THEIR ORIGINAL DIMENSION NOR WITH EACH OTHER.

Drawing three-dimensional objects and furniture

To understand this technique of the projection view, start with simple objects, such as cubes, before drawing spaces. Practise by drawing pieces of furniture or domestic appliances – this is a good exercise which will familiarise you with their shapes and dimensions. These progressive sketches will also remind you of the initial principles of drawing: lines of construction and proportions.

You will notice, looking at the drawings, at which point this view is useful in drawing a small object. This is due to the fact that, if we limit ourselves to a reduced part of the visual field and also away from the vanishing point, the view is practically the same as perspective with vanishing points (see drawing, p67).

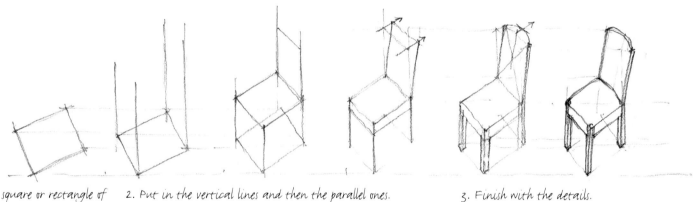

1. Draw the square or rectangle of the ground plan of the object.

2. Put in the vertical lines and then the parallel ones.

3. Finish with the details.

The finished drawing.

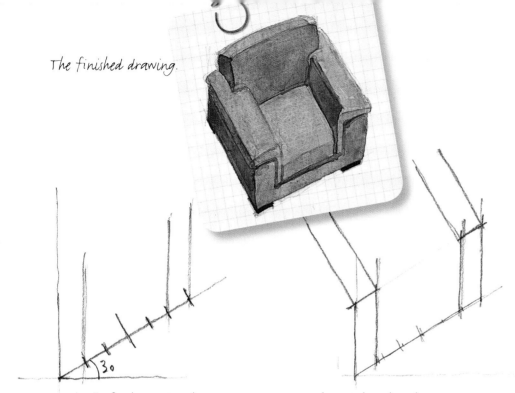

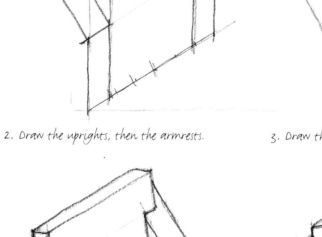

1. Draw an angle of 30°, then divide the top line in two. Then divide each half in three.

2. Draw the uprights, then the armrests.

3. Draw the foot of the sides, then the seat.

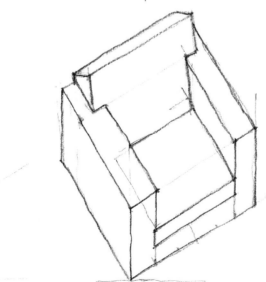

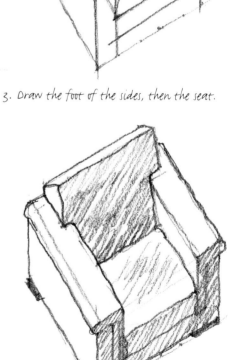

4. Draw the angle of the back

5. Draw the back and then the rest of the arms.

6. Add shading.

Design an office space

Taking advantage of the benefits of the projection view, i.e. keeping the dimensions, make some detailed studies of an object or a small piece of furniture. More visual than ground plans, these studies allow you to show thickness, objects superimposed one upon another and spaces. Thanks to the flexibility of drawing in pencil, we can introduce see-through views, avoiding multiple views of the same thing.

A foldaway office on a shelf

If you only have a small space, and not much money, you can make yourself a foldaway office, even a mobile one if you fit castors on it.

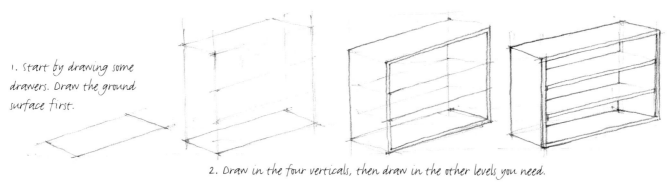

1. Start by drawing some drawers. Draw the ground surface first.

2. Draw in the four verticals, then draw in the other levels you need.

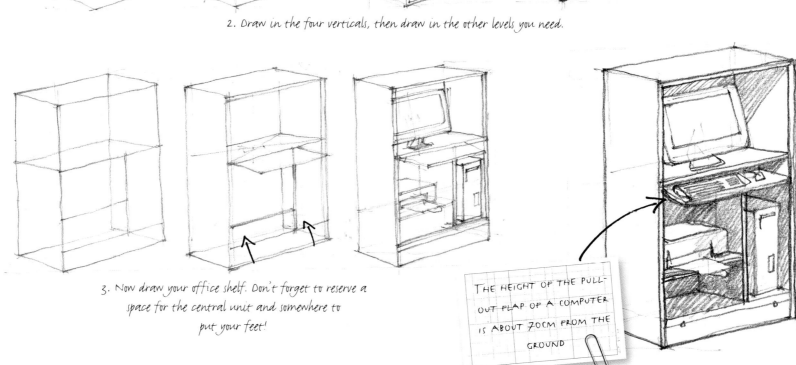

3. Now draw your office shelf. Don't forget to reserve a space for the central unit and somewhere to put your feet!

THE HEIGHT OF THE PULL-OUT FLAP OF A COMPUTER IS ABOUT 70CM FROM THE GROUND

Grouping office furniture

The projection view enables you to move furniture around as you please. Try out some arrangements to find the one that suits you best, before buying the various elements of your office corner.

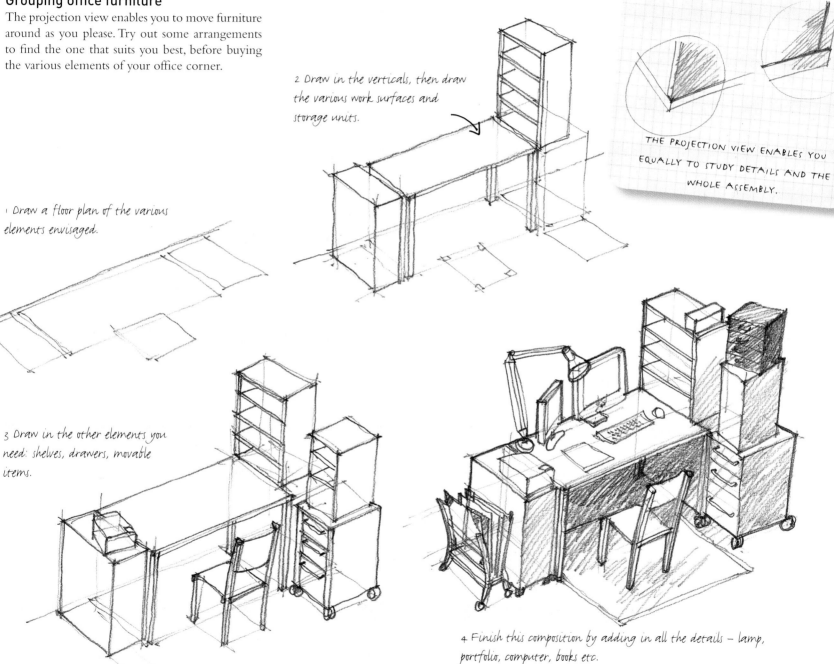

2 Draw in the verticals, then draw the various work surfaces and storage units.

THE PROJECTION VIEW ENABLES YOU EQUALLY TO STUDY DETAILS AND THE WHOLE ASSEMBLY.

1 Draw a floor plan of the various elements envisaged.

3 Draw in the other elements you need: shelves, drawers, movable items.

4 Finish this composition by adding in all the details – lamp, portfolio, computer, books etc.

Playing about with space

Finally, we can consider a space as an association of walls and objects. Using a grid traced out before and placed under the page (if the paper is thin enough) allows you to play about with spaces as you please. Once you have mastered the principles of projection you have at your disposition a highly useful instrument, equivalent to a small-scale model, but easier to modify.

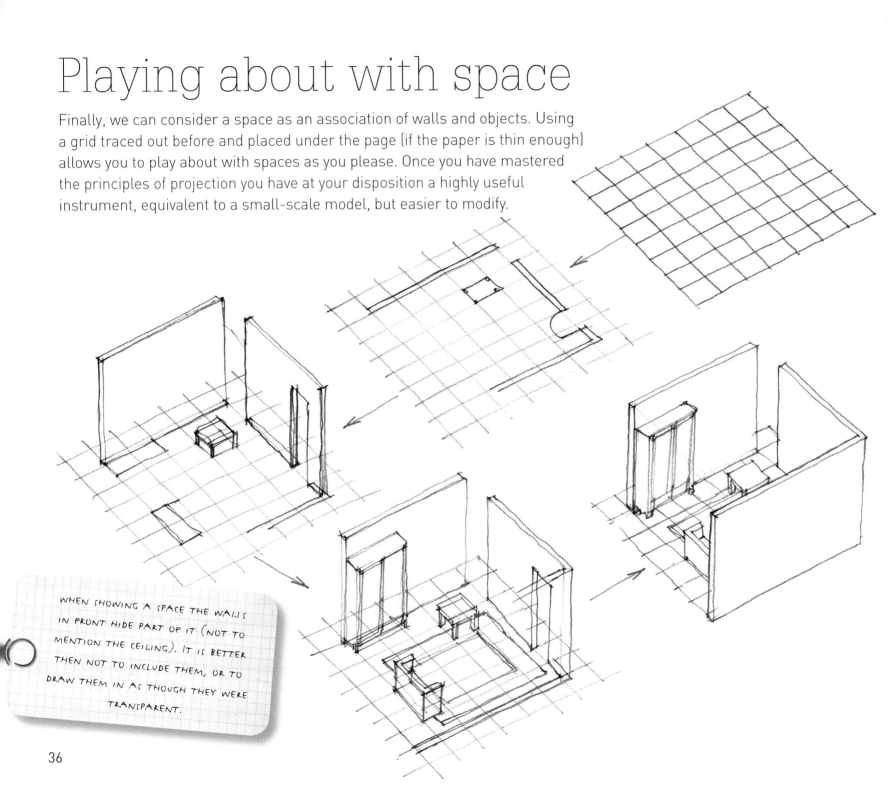

WHEN SHOWING A SPACE THE WALLS IN FRONT HIDE PART OF IT (NOT TO MENTION THE CEILING). IT IS BETTER THEN NOT TO INCLUDE THEM, OR TO DRAW THEM IN AS THOUGH THEY WERE TRANSPARENT.

Drawing a kitchen

Here is an exercise in using projection. The preliminary drawing of the corner of the room and a framework of 60cm squares automatically enables you to place units to the correct size. This visualisation of the units, even if simplified, enables you to group them better.

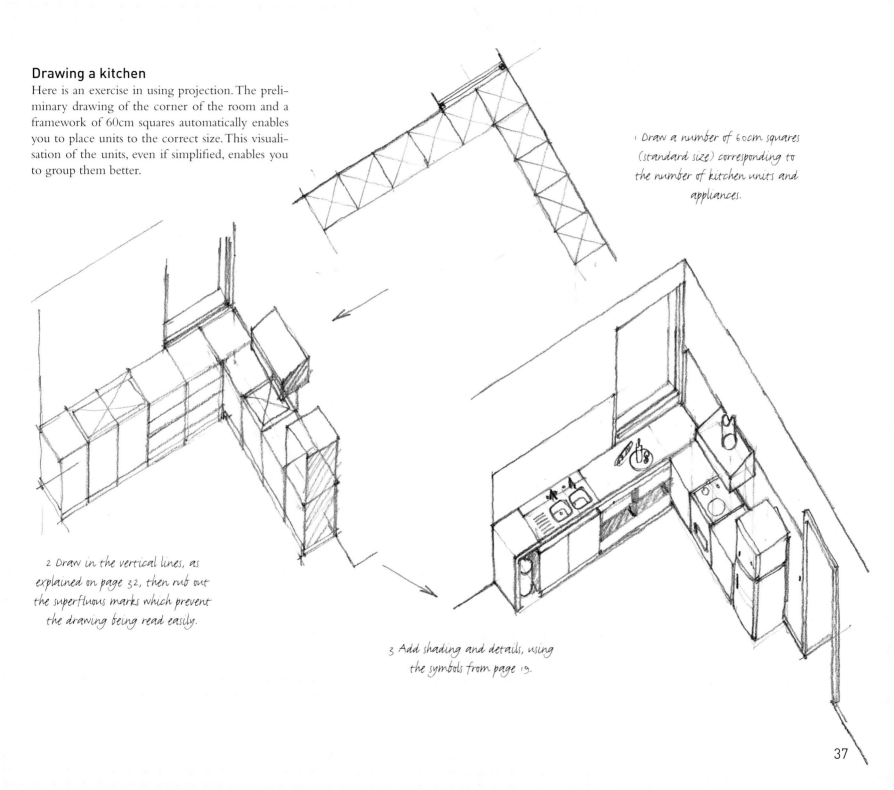

1 Draw a number of 60cm squares (standard size) corresponding to the number of kitchen units and appliances.

2 Draw in the vertical lines, as explained on page 32, then rub out the superfluous marks which prevent the drawing being read easily.

3 Add shading and details, using the symbols from page 19.

Swapping round kitchen and bathroom

This project makes a significant change to the home. In some old flats or houses the kitchen is often far from the dining area and the bathroom is very small. What we want to do is swap them round, creating a kitchen corner in a living-room with a dining area, and a more spacious bathroom with natural light. The living rooms have been enlarged by getting rid of a door and taking down a partition wall. This is shown in the following example, where a layout has already been done (see p.26).

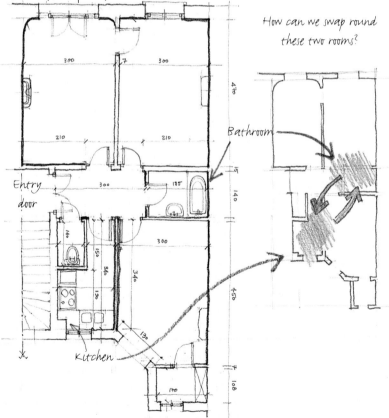

How can we swap round these two rooms?

Bathroom

Entry door

Kitchen

Drawing in projection enables us to see the available space.

The partitions have been taken away so that we can visualise the future kitchen better, but also so we can measure up the demolition work to be done.

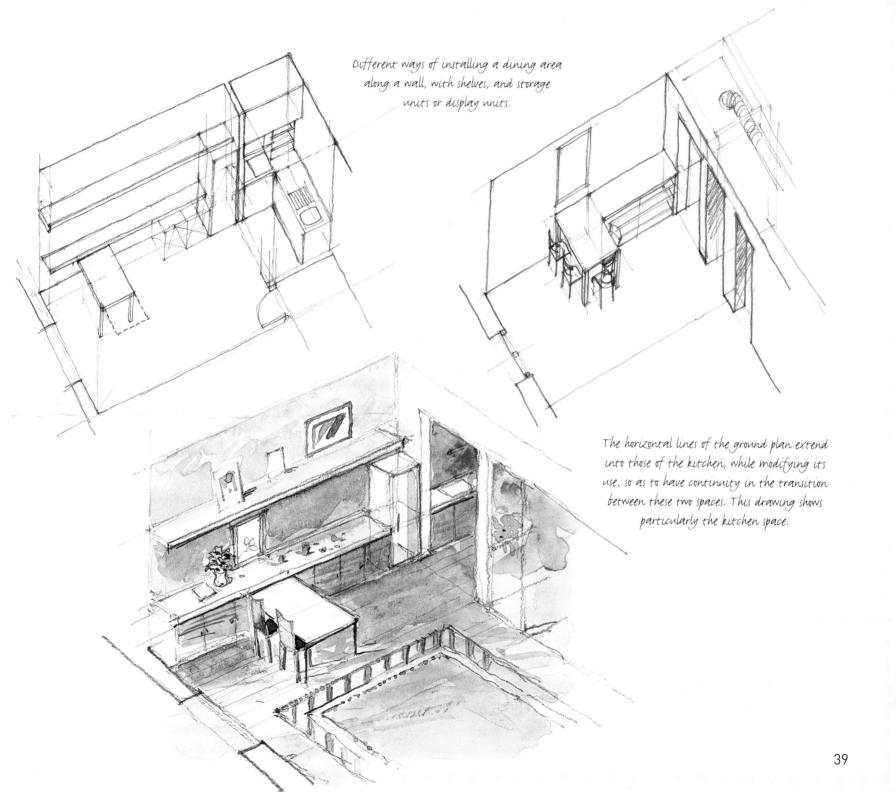

Different ways of installing a dining area along a wall, with shelves, and storage units or display units.

The horizontal lines of the ground plan extend into those of the kitchen, while modifying its use, so as to have continuity in the transition between these two spaces. This drawing shows particularly the kitchen space.

Visualising a kitchen corner

This example, taken from the transformation on page 38, puts into practice the studies made on kitchen furniture, and the different combinations on the 60cm module. The projection view, like other representations, shows here its limitations, because it is impossible to show a space, and the walls which delimit it, at the same time. Only the ground plans and sections in their way give precise solutions to this problem.

However, projections have the advantage of raising questions, like that of the partition wall now separating the kitchen from the entry hall, which was before the wall with the bathroom door. (This partition is studied on p.42.)

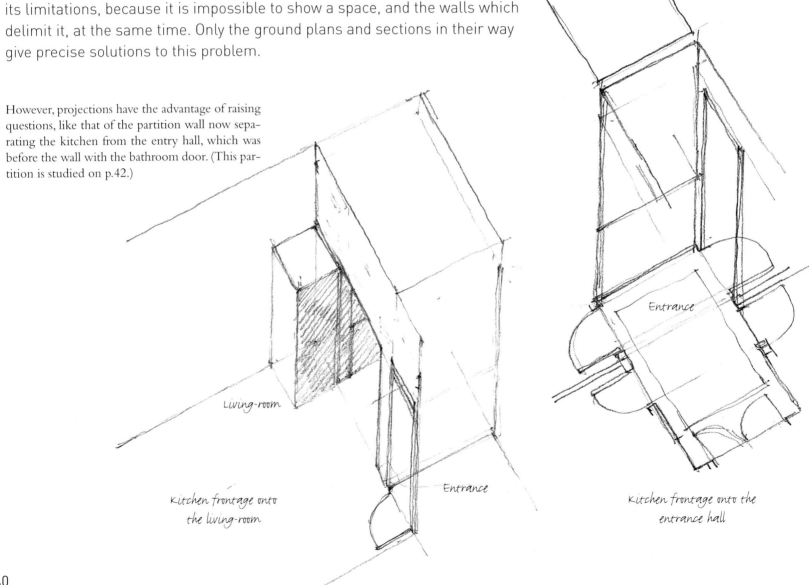

Living-room

Entrance

Entrance

Kitchen frontage onto
the living-room

Kitchen frontage onto the
entrance hall

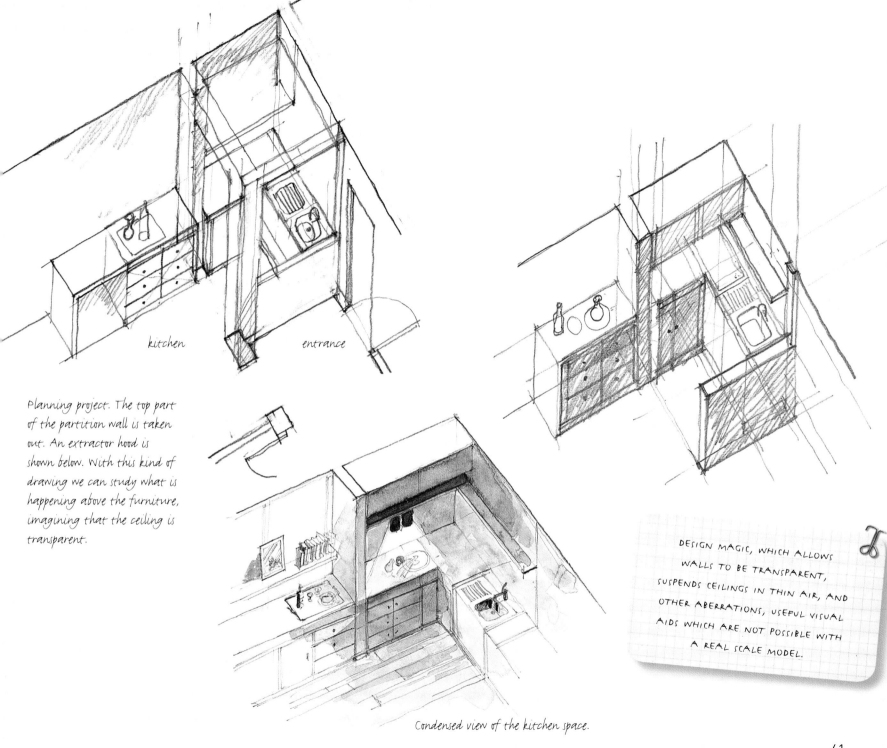

kitchen

entrance

Planning project. The top part of the partition wall is taken out. An extractor hood is shown below. With this kind of drawing we can study what is happening above the furniture, imagining that the ceiling is transparent.

Condensed view of the kitchen space.

DESIGN MAGIC, WHICH ALLOWS WALLS TO BE TRANSPARENT, SUSPENDS CEILINGS IN THIN AIR, AND OTHER ABERRATIONS, USEFUL VISUAL AIDS WHICH ARE NOT POSSIBLE WITH A REAL SCALE MODEL.

Creating an open partition

The reorganising of the space in this flat (see p.40) means that the end of the entry hall acts at the same time as an open partition into the kitchen.

This partition has two distinct parts: top and bottom. The bottom must remain closed because it conceals kitchen elements, equipment or storage. On the other hand the top part can stay open or half-open, in any case becoming the object of an obvious change. The partition becomes the frontage of the kitchen, while still being the end of the entry hall. We can treat it with elements which have some of the properties of a façade, such as louvres, venetian blinds and houseplants.

IF YOU CREATE A SLIDING PARTITION, DON'T FORGET IT WILL HAVE TO BE SUSPENDED!

THE VARIOUS STAGES

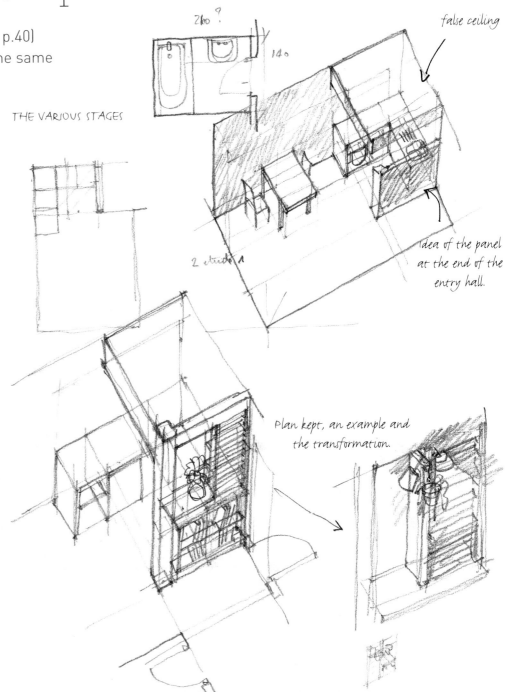

false ceiling

Idea of the panel at the end of the entry hall.

Plan kept, an example and the transformation.

42

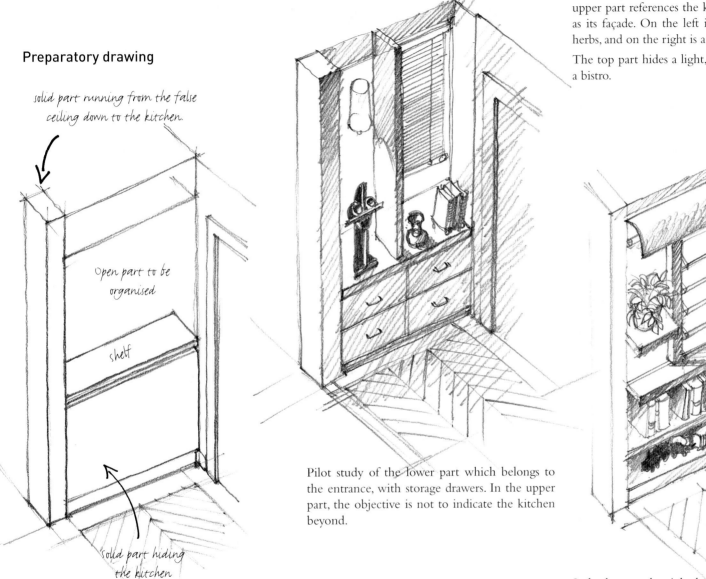

Preparatory drawing

solid part running from the false ceiling down to the kitchen.

Open part to be organised

shelf

solid part hiding the kitchen

Pilot study of the lower part with open shelves. The upper part references the kitchen, and is presented as its façade. On the left is a stand with a pot of herbs, and on the right is a system of louvres.

The top part hides a light, evoking the shutters of a bistro.

Pilot study of the lower part which belongs to the entrance, with storage drawers. In the upper part, the objective is not to indicate the kitchen beyond.

In both cases, the right-hand side is more opaque, to hide the kitchen elements, while on the left it is more open, looking towards the dining area.

Transforming a flat

In this other example, it is a space with a double orientation which will be created in switching round the kitchen and bathroom.

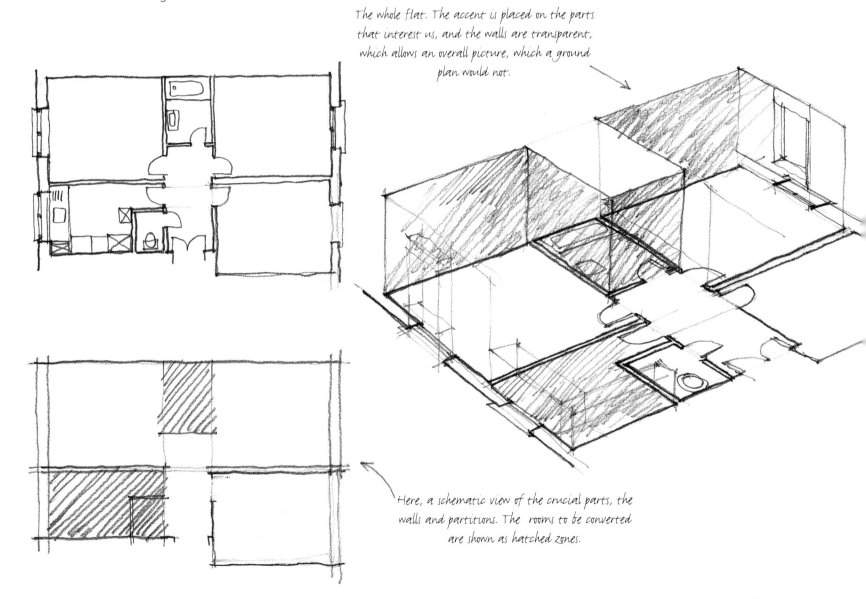

The whole flat. The accent is placed on the parts that interest us, and the walls are transparent, which allows an overall picture, which a ground plan would not.

Here, a schematic view of the crucial parts, the walls and partitions. The rooms to be converted are shown as hatched zones.

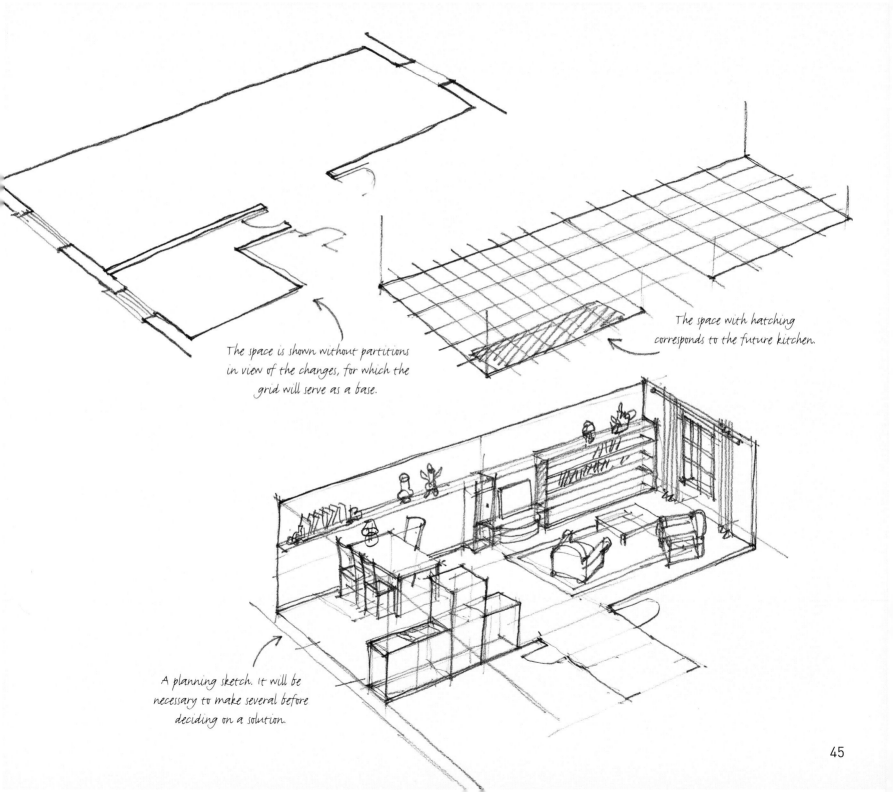

The space is shown without partitions in view of the changes, for which the grid will serve as a base.

The space with hatching corresponds to the future kitchen.

A planning sketch. It will be necessary to make several before deciding on a solution.

45

Creating a dressing-room and a bathroom

Different kinds of spaces can be drawn up very quickly using ready-made grids. Use tracing paper, or any other paper that is transparent enough, to let the markings show through. Below, exploring different uses of a space, using grid 2 (p.83), shown in grey in the first drawing to show it in position.

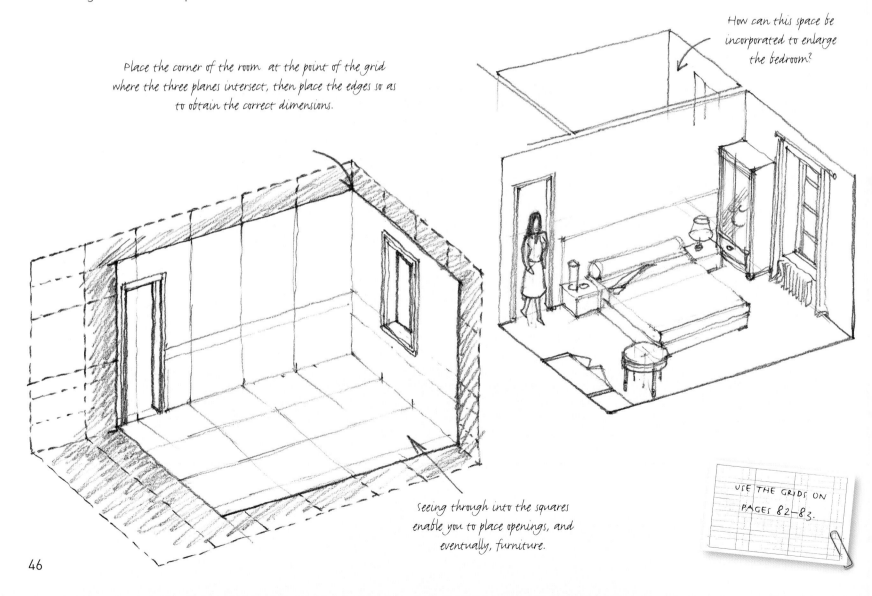

BEFORE

How can this space be incorporated to enlarge the bedroom?

Place the corner of the room at the point of the grid where the three planes intersect, then place the edges so as to obtain the correct dimensions.

seeing through into the squares enable you to place openings, and eventually, furniture.

USE THE GRIDS ON PAGES 82-83.

46

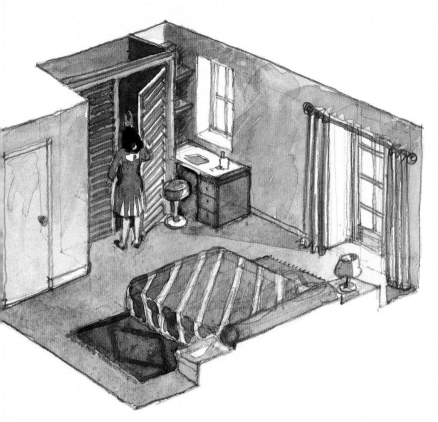

AFTER
The space has been redesigned to create a
dressing-room. The space in front of the window
has been used to design a little office corner.

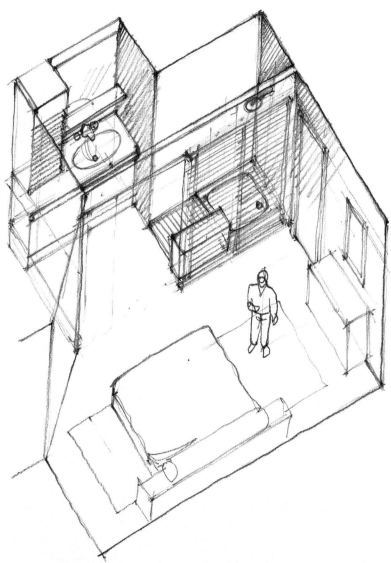

Here, the kitchen has been converted into the bathroom (see p.38).
The corridor which led to the kitchen has been used to create the shower.

Seeing things in perspective

The effect of perspective comes from what our vision makes of what the eye sees. Between the eye and the outlines of an object we can draw the sides of an angle, the angle at which we see the object. We can observe that if the object moves further away, this angle becomes narrower, and to the eye, the object seems to be smaller. This is the effect known as perspective.

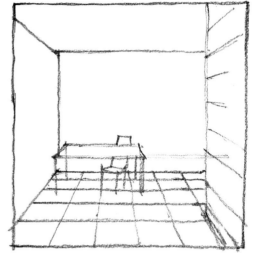

1. The drawing below has been simplified to observe the lines of perspective.

The further away an object is, the smaller it seems.

The vanishing point

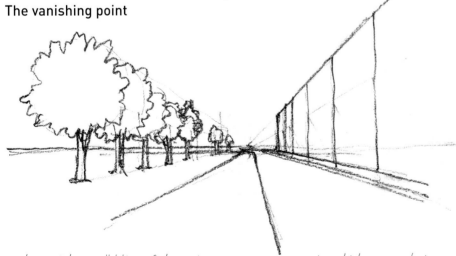

The straight parallel lines of the road appear to meet at a point which seems to be in infinity. This is the vanishing point.

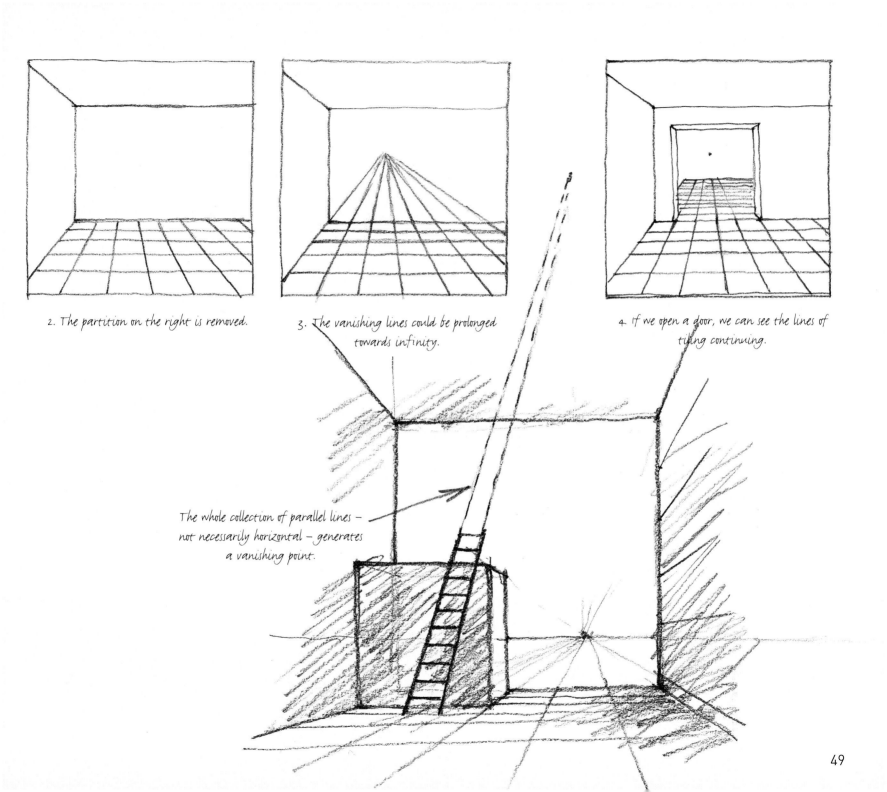

2. The partition on the right is removed.

3. The vanishing lines could be prolonged towards infinity.

4. If we open a door, we can see the lines of tiling continuing.

The whole collection of parallel lines – not necessarily horizontal – generates a vanishing point.

49

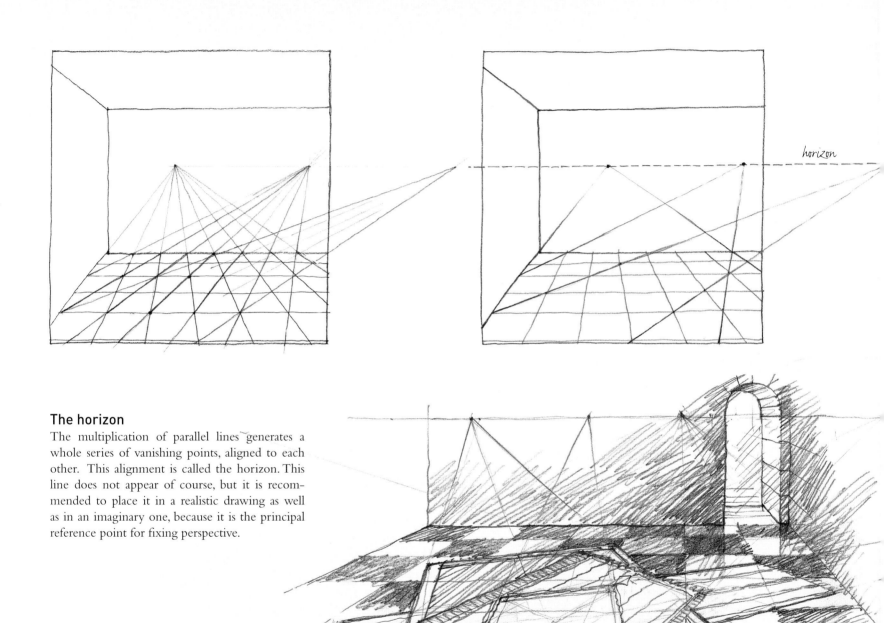

The horizon

The multiplication of parallel lines generates a whole series of vanishing points, aligned to each other. This alignment is called the horizon. This line does not appear of course, but it is recommended to place it in a realistic drawing as well as in an imaginary one, because it is the principal reference point for fixing perspective.

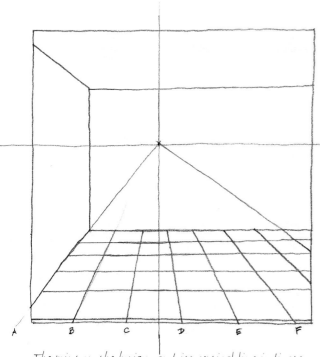

The point on the horizon and its vertical line indicate the position of the observer.

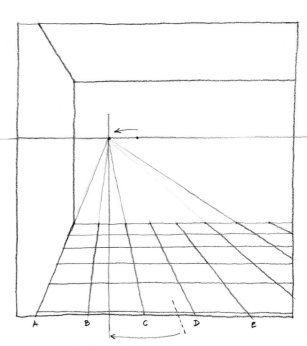

The observer has taken a step to the left.

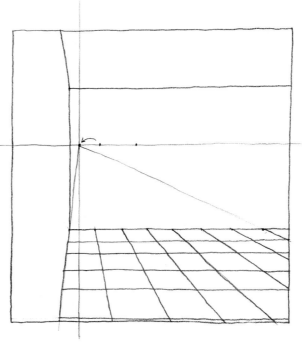

The observer has taken a second step to the left.

Moving the vanishing point on the horizon

When we move, the vanishing point of the lines in one direction seems to move too. We can experience this in a room by looking at the vanishing point of the tiling. This shows that the vanishing point is not just an effect of lines, but also an effect of our vision and our position in a space.

The height of the horizon

Our position in a space affects both the vanishing point and the horizon. In the drawings on this page, look at the view from above and below. They show clearly that the horizon, at the height of the vanishing point, the convergence of the edges of the shelves, is at eye level. And if we stand higher, or sit lower, we can see that the horizon follows our movement.

The height of the horizon in the drawing

Once the height of the horizon has been established in a space, it must be shown in the drawing. That then depends on the framing you want. If you want to show what is above the horizon, you will place it towards the bottom of the window (see p.73).

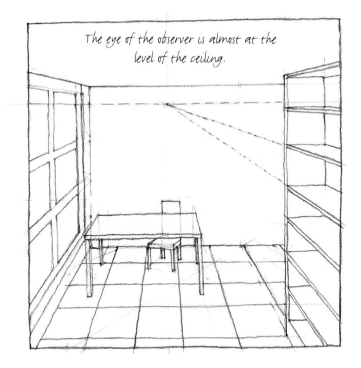

The eye of the observer is almost at the level of the ceiling.

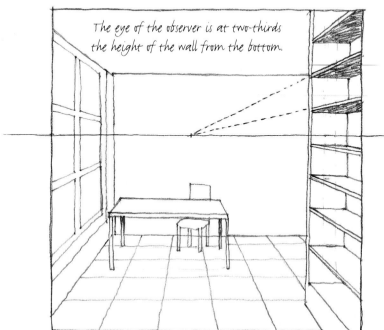

The eye of the observer is at two-thirds the height of the wall from the bottom.

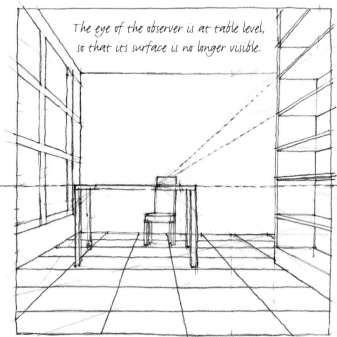

The eye of the observer is at table level, so that its surface is no longer visible.

This man is not only at an impossible height: even his size is impossible. But if the wall becomes transparent, everything becomes in order and the man is in place, much further away.

This woman is not to scale, because her height is not in keeping with the others.

Here we can estimate the height of the room, seeing that the horizon, at eye level, comes about two-thirds up the wall; so the height from the ceiling is about 2.5 metres.

Here the horizon, at eye level, comes about a quarter of a way up the walls. We then see that the room has monumental proportions, with a height of around 6 metres. The man on the right is taller than the observer, because his head is above the line of the horizon.

The height of the horizon, people and the scale

The horizon being at eye level of the observer (about 1.5 metres if he/she is standing) it follows that if other people, positioned in the same way, are shown in the drawing, their eyes will be at the same level, aligned with the horizon. At the same time, this perception can tell us instinctively about the height of the room.

THESE SKETCHES SHOW THAT THE HORIZON IS A VALUABLE INDICATOR IN A DRAWING. EVEN IF IT IS NOT KEPT, TRACING IT OUT IS ESSENTIAL FOR REALISM.

In this drawing, we feel that the observer must be seated, because the horizon is at eye level of the person seated on the right while below the height of the people standing.

53

The view from the front

This is the view facing you, the main part, usually the wall from the bottom, shown in elevation and the sides in perspective. The wall is not distorted by perspective – the sides stay parallel, the proportions are kept and we can choose which scale to use.

FRONTAL VIEWS

Frontal lines

Bottom lines (perpendicular to the wall at the end)

This view presents all the advantages of perspective, and in an architectural drawing of the interior it allows us to show the floor, the side walls and all the elements seen here – furniture and the arrangement of details – in a much more realistic way than a projection.

Moreover, if we take a photo, keeping the axis of the object horizontal and perpendicular to the wall, we get a frontal view.

We have the impression of being in the space shown, while with the projection view we were outside. In principle there is no longer the problem of walls in front hiding things, walls which have to be deleted or made transparent.

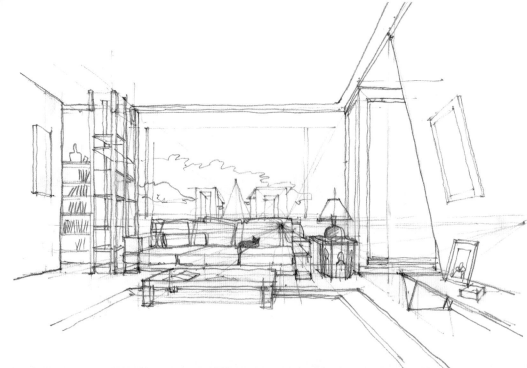

The principles of a frontal view

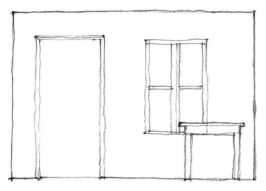

1. Sketch of the panel from the bottom.

2. We define the height of the horizon, which corresponds to the eye level of the observer.

The problem of depth

At this stage there remains one problem: how to define the depth. In effect, nothing allows us to draw the lines in front of or behind the back wall if they are parallel to it. They are at a certain distance, governed by perspective, and we need a way of fixing this distance. In the following pages you will find an exact method of doing this. The principle is simple, but, if geometry is not your thing, the explanation might seem rather abstract. If you want to draw exact perspectives you have to apply it, but for sketchbook studies, which we are mainly interested in here, it is enough to understand the principle, and then apply it by guesswork, in order to avoid obvious errors of perception.

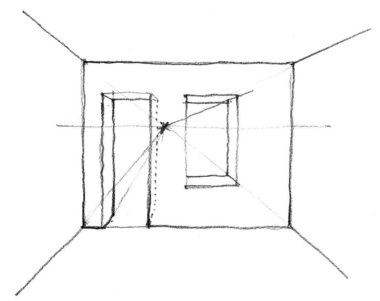

3. We choose a position for the vanishing point on the horizon, centre, left or right, which corresponds to the possible positions of the observer, as we saw earlier (see p.53). We can then draw in the vanishing lines which demarcate the side walls, ceiling etc.

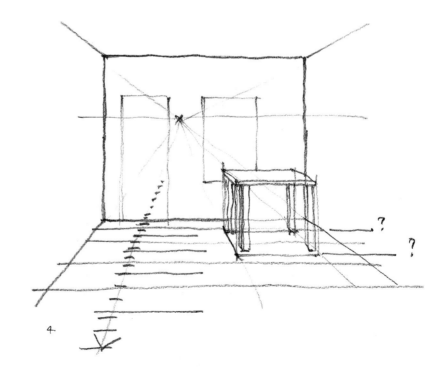

4.

To draw the depth

Here is how to go about drawing the depth of
a frontal view. If you prefer you can just do this
first exercise, which explains the method. It's very
simple – let's start with a small example.

3. Place point D (another vanishing point) on
the horizon to the right, situated at distance
equal to that where you are placed in relation
to the wall. This distance is measured on
the horizon, to the same scale.

1. Draw a back wall to a chosen scale.
Draw in the horizon, the vanishing point O,
and points A and B at the foot of the wall.

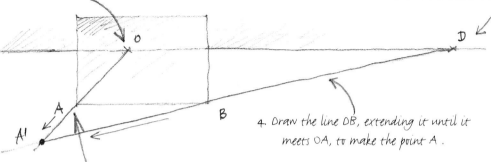

4. Draw the line DB, extending it until it
meets OA, to make the point A .

2. Draw the line OA and
extend it towards the front.

YOU CAN ARRIVE AT THESE
VIEWS IN A MORE INTUITIVE
WAY, AND SO SKIP THIS
EXPLANATION.

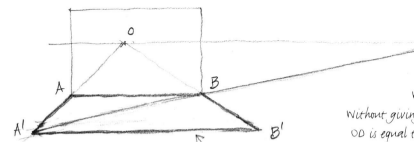

5. Draw the horizontal line A' B', then B B'.
You have marked out on the ground a square,
attached to the back wall.

WHY IS IT A SQUARE?
Without giving a demonstration, note that when
OD is equal to the distance of the observer from
the horizon, D becomes the vanishing point of all
the lines which are at 45° to the ground plan.
A'B makes an angle of 45° and so constitutes the
diagonal of a square. This property enables us to
find the depth from the width.

56

Mastering the depth

You see then that points O and D show your position in the space: point O gives your height and your position laterally; point D gives your distance.

Mastery of the distance is a little tricky. If you are placed too near (if D is placed near O) the sides are very distorted. If you are too far away (if D is further from O) you risk being simply outside the room. Moreover, in that case, point D is often outside the drawing – annoying because you need a wider piece of paper that the area being drawn.

We see a similar problem when taking photographs which necessitate wide angle shots to compensate for the absence of distance.

Here too, there are practical limits which we get round by showing transparent walls. We can also choose to show only the part near the back wall, without trying to give too big a view of the sides.

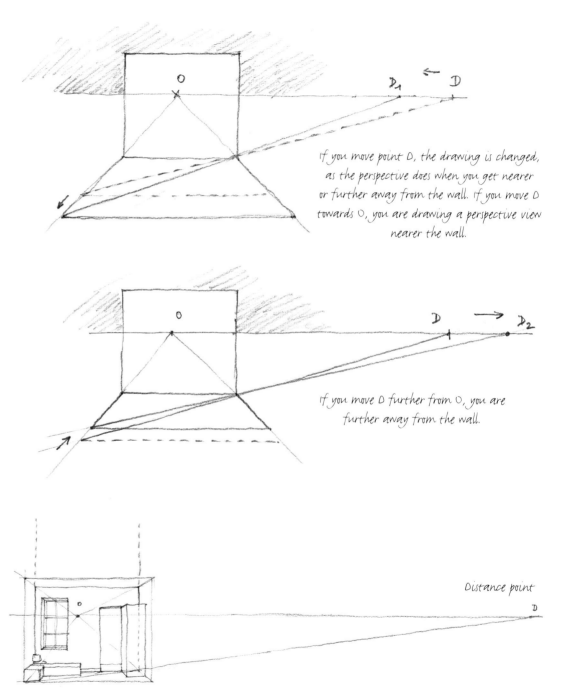

If you move point D, the drawing is changed, as the perspective does when you get nearer or further away from the wall. If you move D towards O, you are drawing a perspective view nearer the wall.

If you move D further from O, you are further away from the wall.

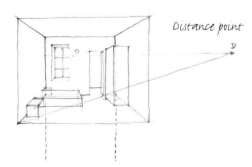

Distance point

Distance point

To move back a partition wall

Here is a simple application of what has just been explained. On the left: a room
in which we propose to move back the partition wall to a certain depth (P). And
on the right: how it will look.

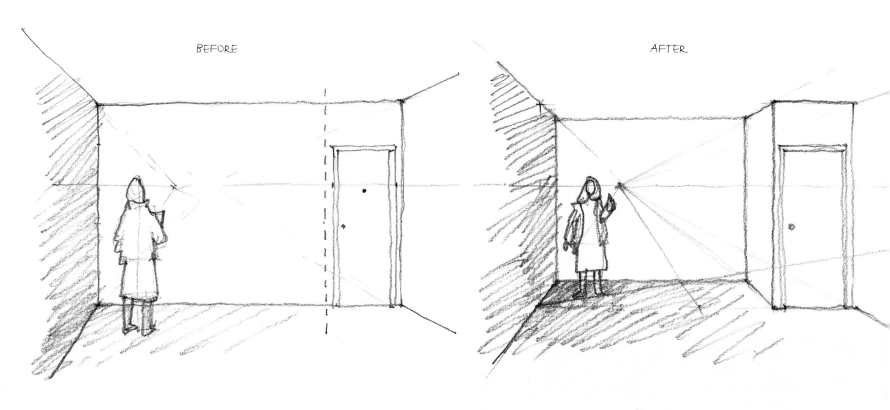

BEFORE

AFTER

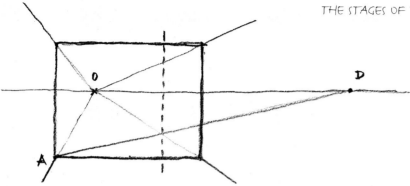

1. Draw the space in elevation, to a given scale. Place the principal vanishing point O. Place the point of distance D, OD corresponding roughly to your distance from the wall. Draw the principal vanishing lines towards O, and one towards D from the bottom angle of the wall at A.

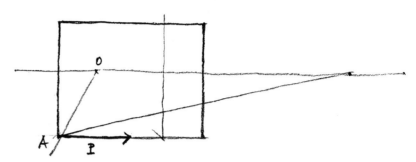

2. From A, mark off a short length AP, equal to P, the required distance the partition has to move.

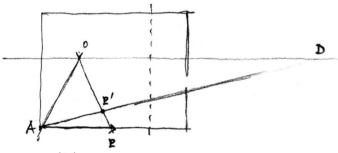

3. Draw PO, which crosses AD at P¹.

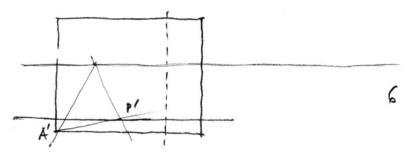

4. Draw on the ground the line A P , which is the base of the new partition wall, applying the principle explained on page 56.

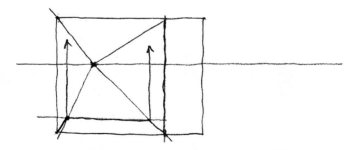

5. Draw in the vertical lines from the base until they intersect with the vanishing lines.

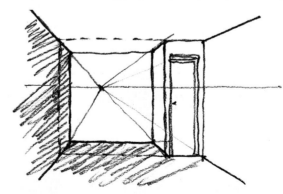

6. Remove the lines no longer needed (left here as dotted lines).

Creating an extension to block off a corner

We can modify the project from p.58 by creating a corner for a home cinema, library, office etc. To do this we have to make an extension from the new partition wall.

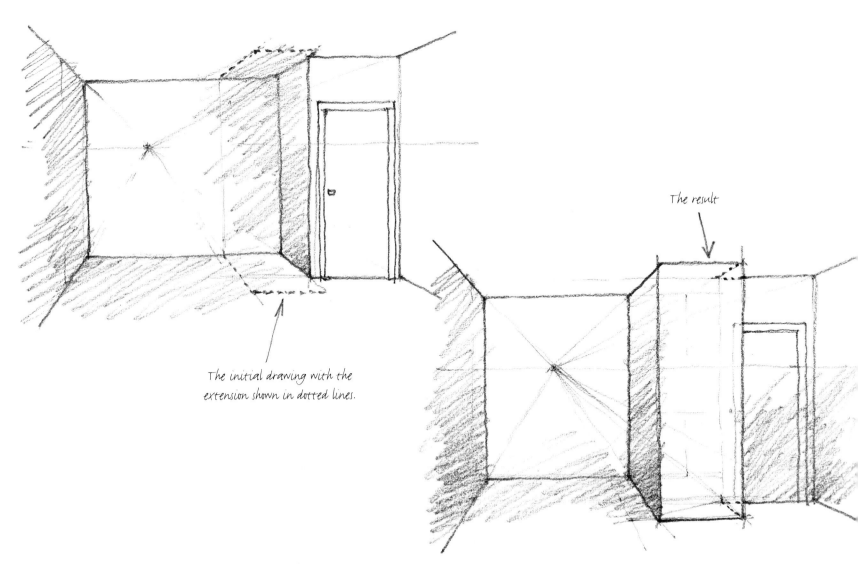

The initial drawing with the extension shown in dotted lines.

The result

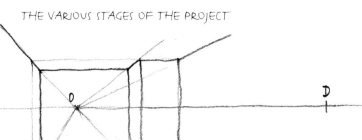

1. We have to go back to the initial sketch of the wall (with one part consisting of the door) because this will enable us to take accurate measurements. In fact, in the perspective drawing, only this ground plan of the partition was drawn to a known scale.

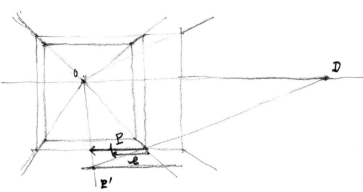

2. Place P (for example P=1.5m, drawn to the scale chosen for the door panel) according to the depth of the extension to be made. Place P on the horizontal, running from the right-hand corner of the door unit. Bring P forward to the middle of the point of distance. You have P'.

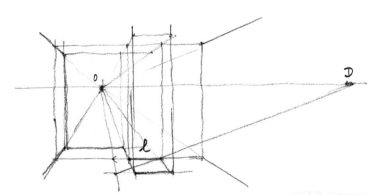

3. Once you have drawn in the back base of the extension, draw in the vertical lines, up to the principal vanishing lines. Then draw the diagonal towards D which will give you the front of the base. Finish by drawing in the vertical lines of the first layout towards the lines of flight.

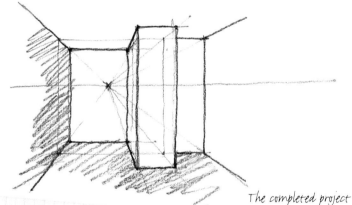

The completed project

BE CAREFUL! DO NOT CONFUSE THE LENGTH P, WHICH GIVES THE DEPTH, AND L, WHICH IS THE WIDTH OF THE NEW EXTENSION.

61

Planning the space

A HOME CINEMA

We can create an extension (see p.60) with the idea of planning a particular space: book corner, child's room, etc.

A BOOK CORNER

The back of the room is used for placing a sofa and shelves. The space turns around the extension/library. The part in front is very open, and contains a work surface and a partition which creates a real little entrance.

The extension is reduced to a partition 1 metre wide which serves to partially isolate and separate a home cinema corner from the rest of the room.

A BEDROOM /OFFICE

The extension is completely closed on the door side and houses bunk beds. The back of the room is turned into an office.

Converting a space under the eaves

How do you draw the perspective of sloping walls and a little flight of steps? In this example it is not the end panel that will be used for the elevation, but an imaginary plan of reference, situated on the first ground plan and symbolised by the dotted line. The point D can thus be placed quite near the O (see p.58) as this project is situated inside the space marked out with the dotted line, and so there is not much danger of distortion.

(see p.58)

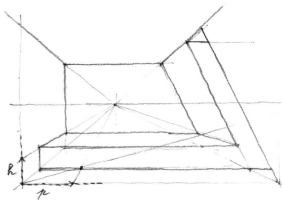

BEFORE
The space before conversion. The plan of reference is symbolised by the dotted line.

Designing a platform for a bed

Choose the height of the platform (50cm) which you place on the left, on the dotted line. The extension P is there so that the platform aligns with the first skylight on the right.

AFTER

Designing a small flight of steps

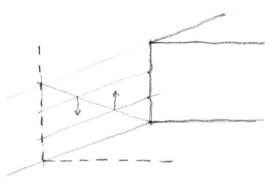

The height (50cm) allows for 3 steps up. We divide the height in three, then draw in the vanishing lines, and by means of the diagonal on the left, divide the horizontals in three to create the risers. The play of the vanishing points and the parallel lines allows us to draw the steps.

Designing a skylight

The second conversion is the creation of a second dormer window on the right-hand wall, at the bottom of the room, which we imagine as being one-third the size of the remaining panel, and in the centre. Here is the method for dividing a panel into three equal parts; it applies equally well to a panel seen in perspective.

Draw the two diagonals of the panel which separates the first dormer window from the end wall. These diagonals give you the middle of the panel. Draw the median line.

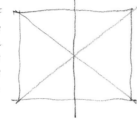

Draw the diagonals of the 2 demi-rectangles thus created.

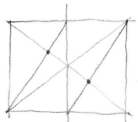

O

At the points of intersection draw the 2 verticals which will divide the panel in three.

1/3   1/3   1/3

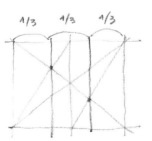

D

THIS METHOD, APPLIED TO PANELS ON A SLOPE, ENABLES US TO FIND THE EXACT WIDTH OF THE OPENING TO BE MADE.

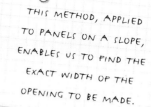

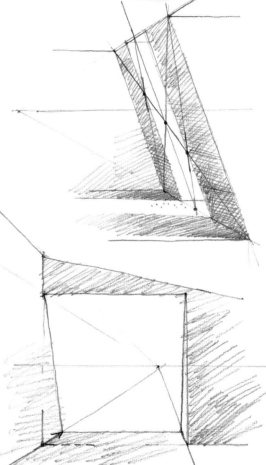

The dormer at the end uses the residual slope of the eaves. To draw it, you have to draw out an extension on the ground (see p.60) and join up the foot and the top of this opening. Then draw an opening in the created panel.

H

L

A few simple construction tricks

How do you establish equal depths?

How do you divide the vanishing line AB into a given number of equal parts (here 5)?

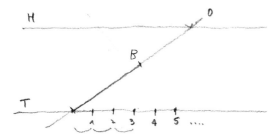

1. Draw a line parallel to the horizon, starting at A, and mark out 5 equal segments.

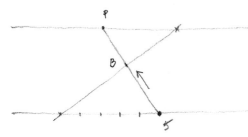

2. Join the last point 5 to point B, and extend it to the horizon line, creating vanishing point P.

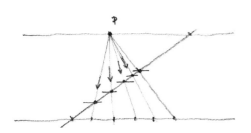

3. Draw lines from P to the points 1, 2, 3 and 4. These vanishing lines divide AB equally.

To divide a wall

It's enough to draw the vertical lines linking T to H.

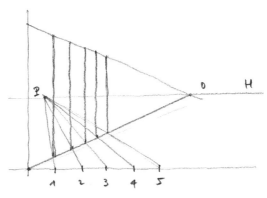

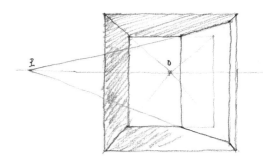

The wall can be divided directly working from a vertical line.

How to deal with an irregular-shaped space

In this space, the right-hand wall has been rotated so that it is no longer perpendicular to the wall below, but turns at an angle. In this case the edges of the panel do not meet at the vanishing point O, but at a new vanishing point P. It's there no matter which horizontal generates a vanishing point on the horizon. This prepares us for the the oblique view in which our gaze, turned to the side, brings about the displacement of the vanishing points.

How do you draw a circle?

The drawing of a circle is always bounded by a square and appears as an ellipse. Note that the large axe and the small axe of the ellipse do not merge with the axes of the square.

Perspective or projection view?

Note that a detail far away from the vanishing point looks like a projection – the vanishing lines are almost parallel. In fact, small objects often appear as if projections. It's why assembly instructions are often illustrated on this principle.

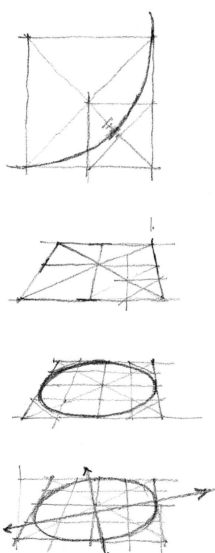

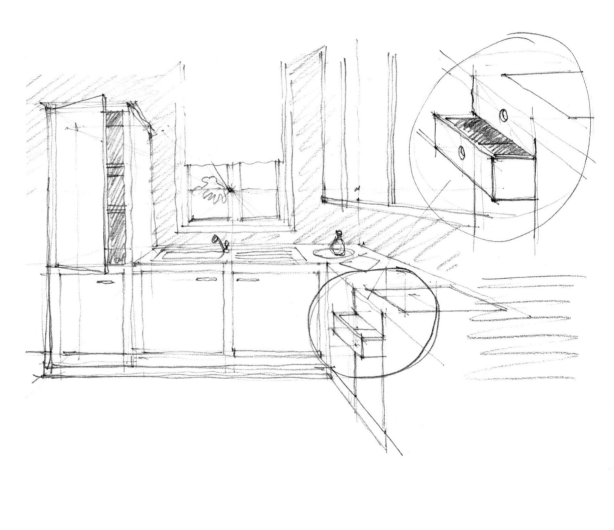

Taking down a partition wall

Different kinds of spaces can be rapidly sketched out by means of a ready-made grid. Work with tracing paper, or any other paper fine enough to show the grid underneath.

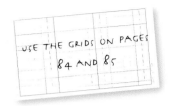

USE THE GRIDS ON PAGES 84 AND 85

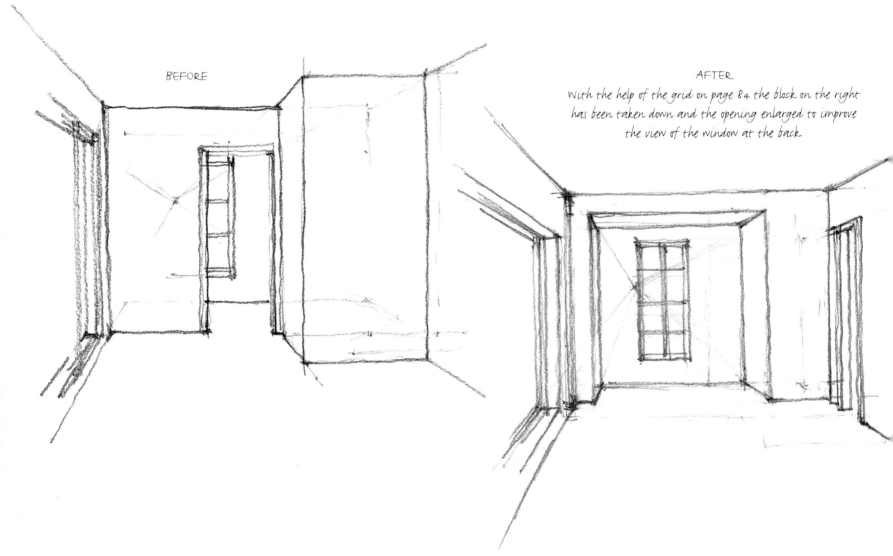

BEFORE

AFTER
With the help of the grid on page 84 the block on the right has been taken down and the opening enlarged to improve the view of the window at the back.

Creating a mezzanine or overhang

Grid 1 (see p.82) allows the study of a more complicated conversion, to take advantage of extra space that has just been created at the end of a room.

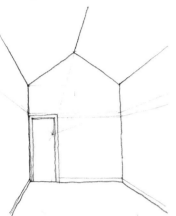

BEFORE

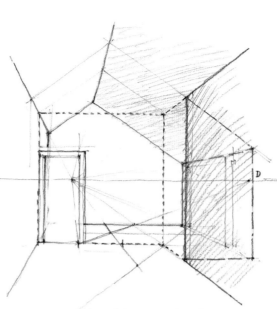

Construction lines help us visualise the new space. This was not visible in the first sketch.

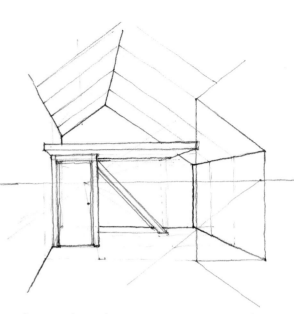

The principles of this conversion: a platform on the mezzanine floor and a staircase/ladder. The door on the left is to stay, but will be slightly built over by the platform. We can gauge the effect of the future mezzanine.

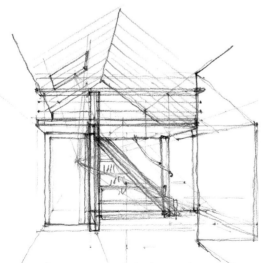

Possible treatment of the handrails and the supporting structure of the platform, to consider their visual impact on the room.

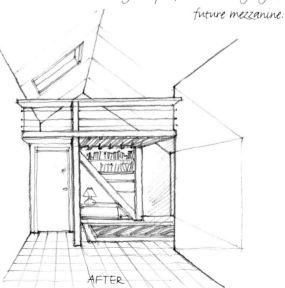

AFTER

69

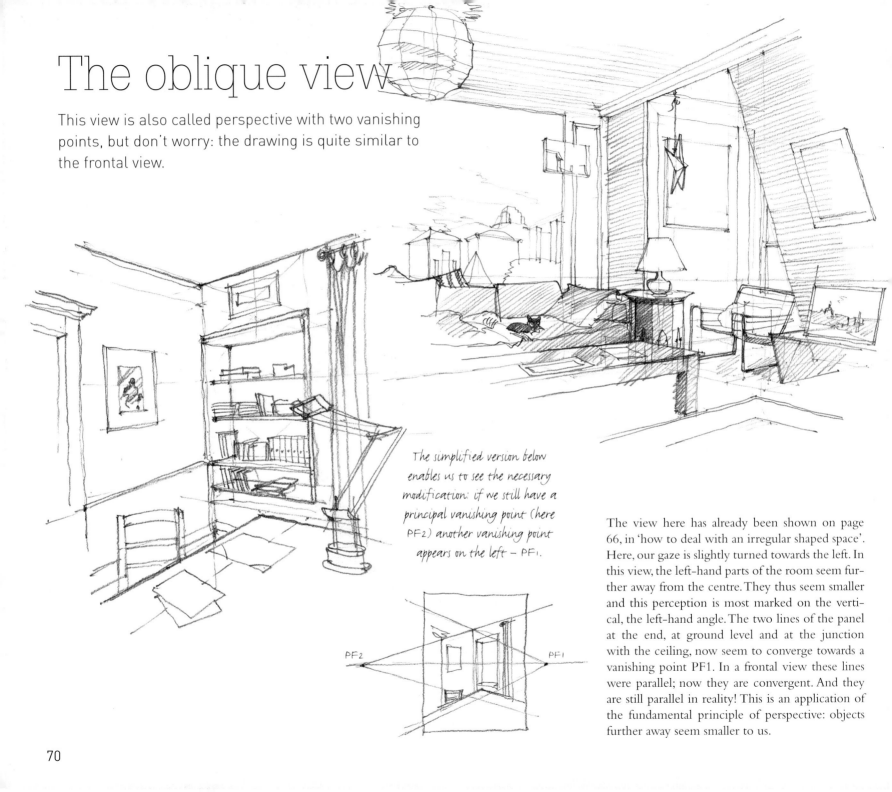

The oblique view

This view is also called perspective with two vanishing points, but don't worry: the drawing is quite similar to the frontal view.

The simplified version below enables us to see the necessary modification: if we still have a principal vanishing point (here PF2) another vanishing point appears on the left – PF1.

PF2   PF1

The view here has already been shown on page 66, in 'how to deal with an irregular shaped space'. Here, our gaze is slightly turned towards the left. In this view, the left-hand parts of the room seem further away from the centre. They thus seem smaller and this perception is most marked on the vertical, the left-hand angle. The two lines of the panel at the end, at ground level and at the junction with the ceiling, now seem to converge towards a vanishing point PF1. In a frontal view these lines were parallel; now they are convergent. And they are still parallel in reality! This is an application of the fundamental principle of perspective: objects further away seem smaller to us.

The rigorous construction of this kind of perspective necessitates a ground plan, an elevation or a section and a geometric device which is a little complicated and which is not shown here. Nowadays, in professional practice this classic perspective is done by computer (see p.80).

Using the oblique view here starts with a sketch of the ground plan of your interior space or an imaginary space, in which the first elements are placed by guesswork. It's what we call in the following pages 'building by eye'. We also use some tricks of the trade which are enough to obtain a good result.

Here too, the grids enable you to make some sketches (see p.86)

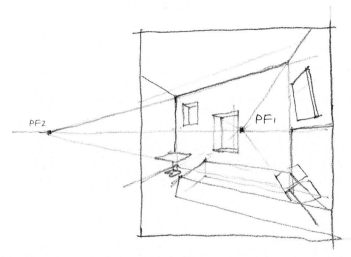

PF2   PF1

ONCE AGAIN WE TURN TOWARDS THE CORNER OF THE ROOM, AND, IF WE PLACE OURSELVES EXACTLY ON THE DIAGONAL, THE TWO VANISHING POINTS ARE PLACED SYMMETRICALLY IN RELATION TO THE CORNER.

71

Designing a room by eye

To design by eye, follow the approach suggested here: setting the boundaries, positioning the horizon and drawing in the principal lines.

The directions of the two vanishing points are perpendicular (90°). You can see distortions forming on the sides and ahead: much better to choose a more moderate angle, using a little guesswork.

Setting the boundaries

Mark out the boundaries of the space you want to show and study: left, right, above and in front of you. Try to avoid too wide an angle - 90° is about the widest angle that our eyes can take in. For the record, an angle of 75° corresponds in photography to an objective with a focus of 24mm, i.e. a very wide angle.

Placing the horizon

The horizon, as you know, is at eye level. To position it well, aim for a point that you are certain is at eye level, then measure it, remembering that the eye level of someone standing is 1.5–1.6 metres high, and 1 metre for someone sitting down. Aim for this point and mentally trace the horizontal line that passes through it. Imagine drawing a red line on the wall at this height. That's the horizon exactly (so long as you don't change height!). When you are drawing, think of putting the horizon, according to the composition you want.

The horizon in the room is at eye level, but on the page it is at the height you choose, according to what you want to show. Generally, it is around the middle.

72

How do you place the horizon in the drawing?

If you are looking upwards, the horizon will be at the bottom of the page.

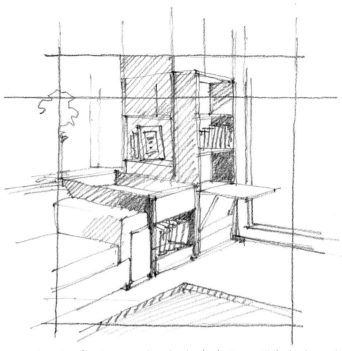

If you are drawing furniture at floor level, the horizon will be high up the page. (Note that if you are looking completely upwards or downwards you are changing the kind of view – we will discuss this later, see p. 78.)

Placing the angles and the line of the ceiling

When you are standing in a room, the most obvious lines are the vertical lines of the corners and the horizontals which mark out the ceiling, like the cornices. Draw these three (or five) lines, being careful with the horizontals of the ceiling, for you still don't know their vanishing point.

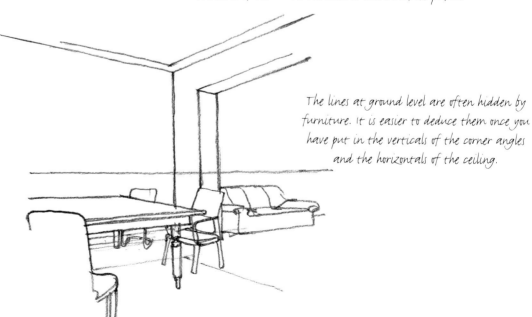

The lines at ground level are often hidden by furniture. It is easier to deduce them once you have put in the verticals of the corner angles and the horizontals of the ceiling.

73

Placing the vanishing point

Now is the moment to put in vanishing points, to left and right. One often feels it would be easy to place them by eye, directly. Experience teaches that this impression is wrong, and leads to mistakes. What I am giving here is an absolutely reliable way of placing the vanishing point:

Take a pencil and hold it horizontal, parallel to the lines where you are looking for the vanishing point. Think of the lines behind you – on the floor or carpet under your feet, or under the furniture – which are often parallel to the first vanishing lines.

Now think of the line from your eye which is going in the same direction. It's one of the family of lines for which you are searching the vanishing point. If you are looking in this direction you are aiming at the vanishing point.

Bring up the pencil to your eye, without changing direction, as if it were a blowpipe with which you are sending a dart towards the point. The point you are aiming at is the vanishing point.

You will probably be surprised to see that the point is not at all where you would have placed it by guesswork, but still further. You will also see that using guesswork you don't put it at the right height on the horizon, but a little above. Generally speaking, one 'sees' the horizon a little too high.

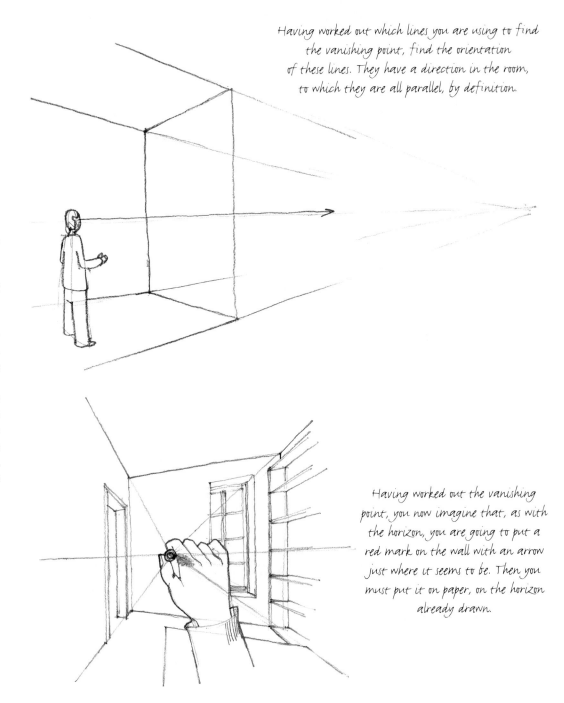

Having worked out which lines you are using to find the vanishing point, find the orientation of these lines. They have a direction in the room, to which they are all parallel, by definition.

Having worked out the vanishing point, you now imagine that, as with the horizon, you are going to put a red mark on the wall with an arrow just where it seems to be. Then you must put it on paper, on the horizon already drawn.

74

If the vanishing point is not on the paper

Very often the vanishing point is outside the composition, and so outside the drawing, or even the sheet of paper. But that doesn't mean outside your vision, even if you have to turn your head slightly to the side. Nevertheless, in so doing you are changing the line of sight and the drawing. In this case you have to be able to draw the lines without the vanishing point. In general we get by using guesswork, but I am going to show you a trick for making another vanishing line, or at least for checking that your drawing is not too inaccurate.

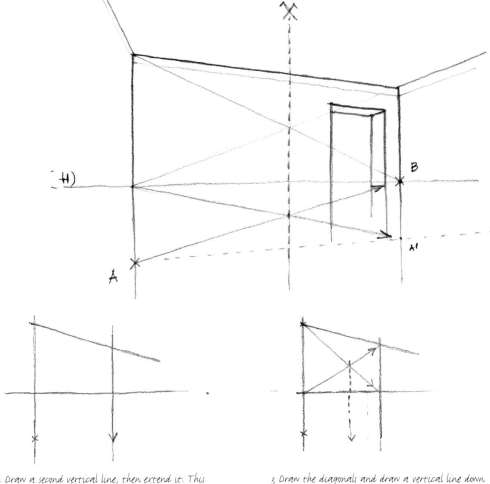

THE STAGES OF CONSTRUCTION

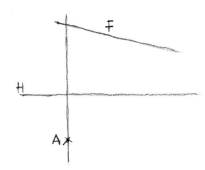

1. Start with a vanishing line F and the horizon H. To draw another vanishing line, from some point A, draw the vertical line which passes through A.

2. Draw a second vertical line, then extend it. This forms a rectangle in perspective.

3. Draw the diagonals and draw a vertical line down from the middle of the rectangle at the point of intersection of the diagonals.

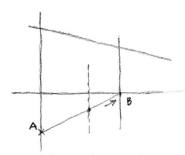

4. Draw AB which crosses this median line.

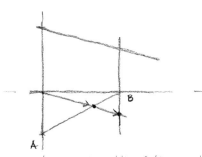

5. Draw the second diagonal line of this rectangle.

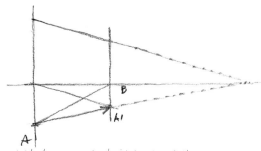

6. Finish the construction by joining A and A'.

75

Different oblique views

Work with tracing paper, or paper thin enough to see the markings underneath. The three examples show how different views of a room can be made using ready-made grids, giving a corner view, the vanishing lines and the dimensions.

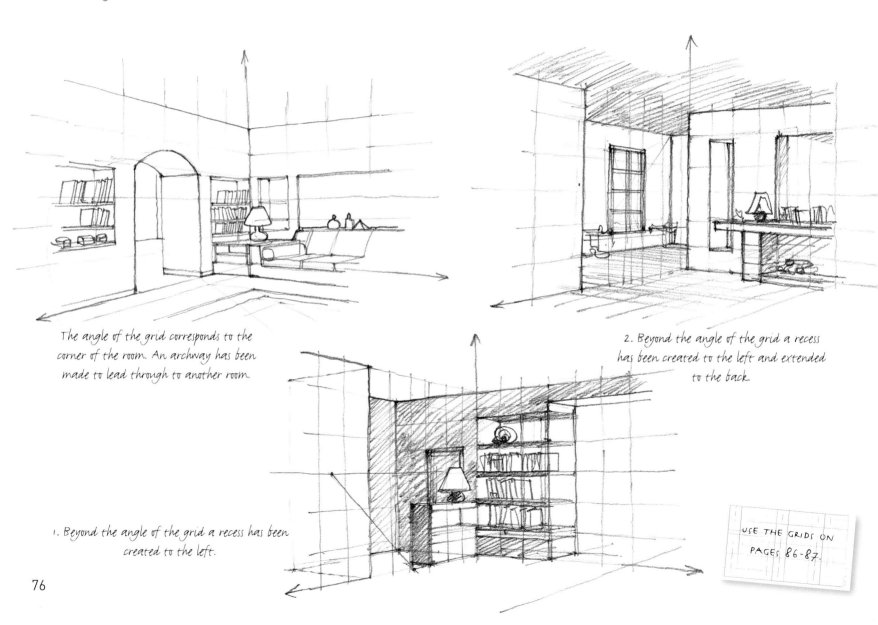

The angle of the grid corresponds to the corner of the room. An archway has been made to lead through to another room.

2. Beyond the angle of the grid a recess has been created to the left and extended to the back.

1. Beyond the angle of the grid a recess has been created to the left.

USE THE GRIDS ON PAGES 86-87.

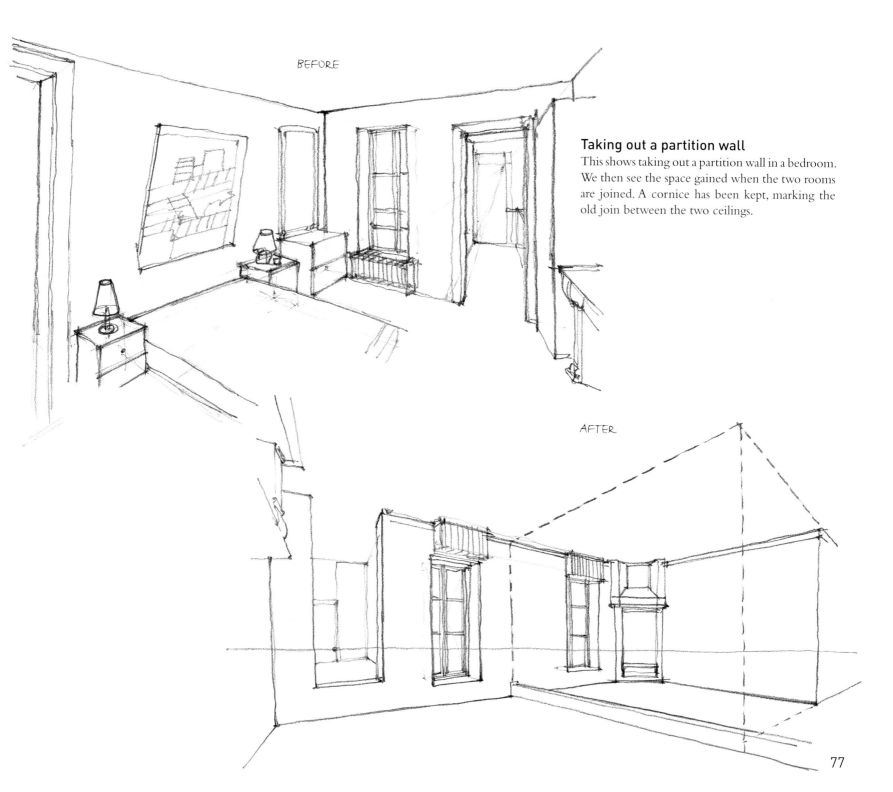

BEFORE

Taking out a partition wall

This shows taking out a partition wall in a bedroom. We then see the space gained when the two rooms are joined. A cornice has been kept, marking the old join between the two ceilings.

AFTER

77

A view from above . . .

Until now we have always assumed a horizontal view, allowing us to see real vertical lines and draw parallels and verticals. This is the view that corresponds to the most usual situation and simplifies drawing in perspective.

 If the sight line is changed dramatically, up or down, the view is transformed. How does the perspective change when the view is not horizontal?

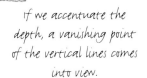

If we accentuate the depth, a vanishing point of the vertical lines comes into view.

The view is still horizontal, with the horizon at the top of the drawing, which allows us to orientate the view towards the bottom.

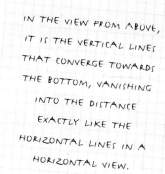

IN THE VIEW FROM ABOVE, IT IS THE VERTICAL LINES THAT CONVERGE TOWARDS THE BOTTOM, VANISHING INTO THE DISTANCE EXACTLY LIKE THE HORIZONTAL LINES IN A HORIZONTAL VIEW.

. . . and a high-angle view

With the high-angle view, the effect is exactly the same upwards.
The drawing shows the same progression.

Horizontal view with the horizon placed
low (here it is outside the drawing.)

The same view, the gaze turned upwards. The
vertical lines begin to converge.

The view called zenithal, or overhead. The vanishing point
situated at the vertical is the point of the sky known as
the zenith.

IN THE HIGH-ANGLE VIEW, IT IS THE
VERTICAL LINES WHICH CONVERGE
AND EXTEND UPWARDS.

79

Drawing on the computer

There are numerous drawing aids available, especially for studying interior design. One way is to take some photos and then trace an outline of the planned modifications. Here is another way that allows you to visualise your interior in 3D, by making a model on the computer.

SketchUp

This is a modelling software program for Macs or PCs, perhaps the most impressive and user-friendly, used by thousands of students and professionals alike. And what's more, it's free. Tap Sketchup into your search engine and follow the instructions. Download the free version and start.

Exploration

You are presented with talking icons, and many aids are available. We show here a small, simple example to show you what it can do, but remember that in spite of its apparent simplicity it is in fact extremely sophisticated. You can make a model, modify it, view it from every angle, add colours and materials, study shadows according to time and place, etc. The online aids are very good - they will help you save a lot of time and discover possibilities you might not otherwise know about.

First steps

Start by exploring the different menus. Later, you can consult the help and download the instruction videos. You will see the ground, bounded by axes, the menu bar and the palette of icons opposite (if not, under Display, choose tools). Here is how to use them for the first time:

Click on 1 (at the bottom) and then on the screen, and then, holding down the mouse button you can move about your space. The little hand enables you to move things sideways. You leave a tool by clicking on the space bar or on the black arrow at the top of the palette.

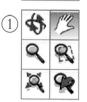

Next, go up the tool palette and click on square 2. Click on the screen, slide across, then click again to let go. You have drawn a rectangle.

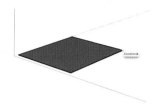

Now click on square 3 – the cursor become a little block with an arrow. Go back to the rectangle which becomes greyish, click on it and then, holding down the button, slide towards the top – a miracle!

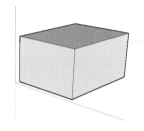

For more fun click on the little box opposite (in the menus at the top) or go to Windows, Shadows, click on 'apply shadows' – another miracle.

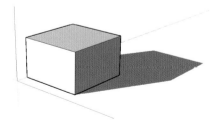

These exercises will show you how SketchUp works. You won't have understood everything, and you need several hours to get used ot it. (Start by printing the 'memento' in the Help menu.)

Making a model for your projects

When you have grasped the main principles, especially the possibility of grouping elements or objects and stipulating their dimensions (see the little box below to the right of the screen) you can use the software for various tasks, seeing the result more or less complete and realistic.

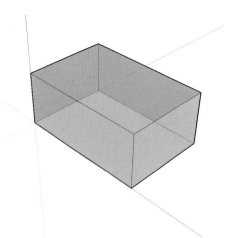

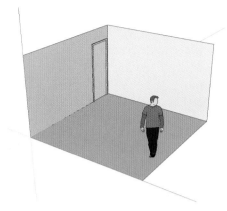

The pictures opposite show the creation of an extension (see pages 60-61).

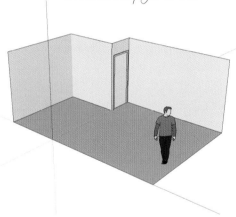

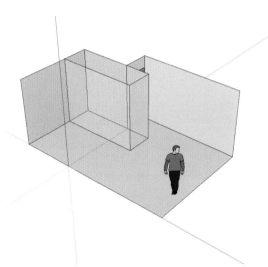

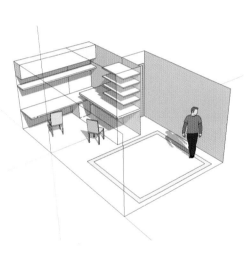

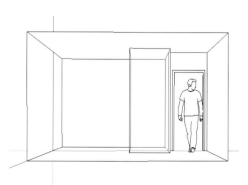

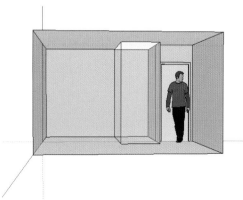

YOU CAN LINK THIS WITH YOUR DRAWING, USING A PENCIL SKETCH TO CREATE IDEAS, THEN BUILDING THEM WITH SKETCHUP, ADDING PERSPECTIVES AND MAKING MODIFICATIONS, AS WITH A PHOTO.

81

Grids for isometric projections

You can use the grids by means of a scanner and printer, or photocopier. The lines are thick so that they show up under tracing paper or a 60gm paper. The two grids show the different angles, which you will recognise. If you slide them under your paper, they will give you the main outlines.

The dotted horizontal lines are the markers. Starting from the bottom, they indicate the height of a bench or chair, then that of a table. The top marker (on grid 2) indicates 2.5 metres, the standard height of a ceiling.

The squares are assumed to be 1 metre (grid 2), but you can use them as 50cm (grid 1) or any other measure which suits you.

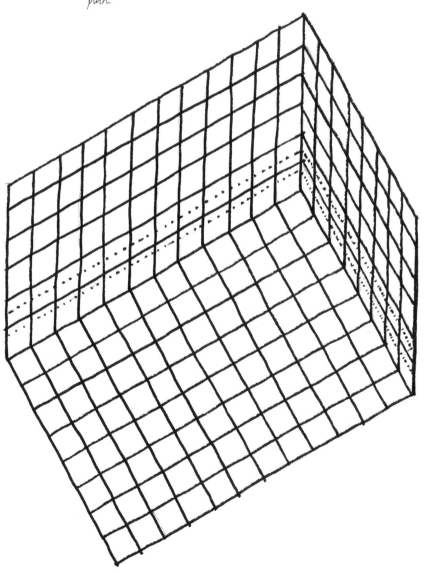

GRID 1

A high-angle view, favouring the ground plan.

GRID 2
View favouring the elevation of the main wall.

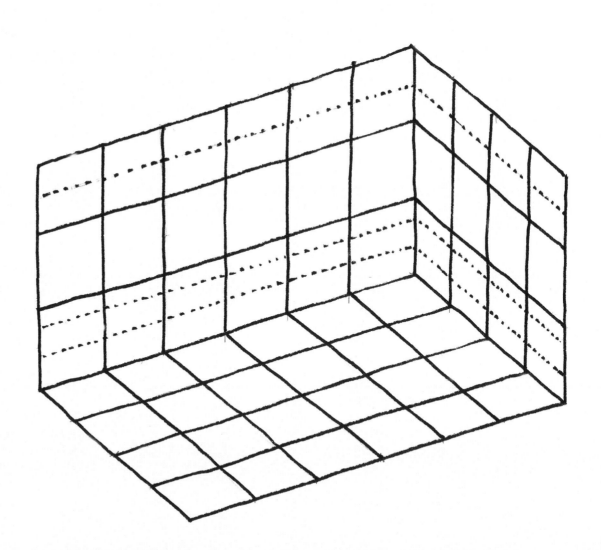

Grids for frontal views

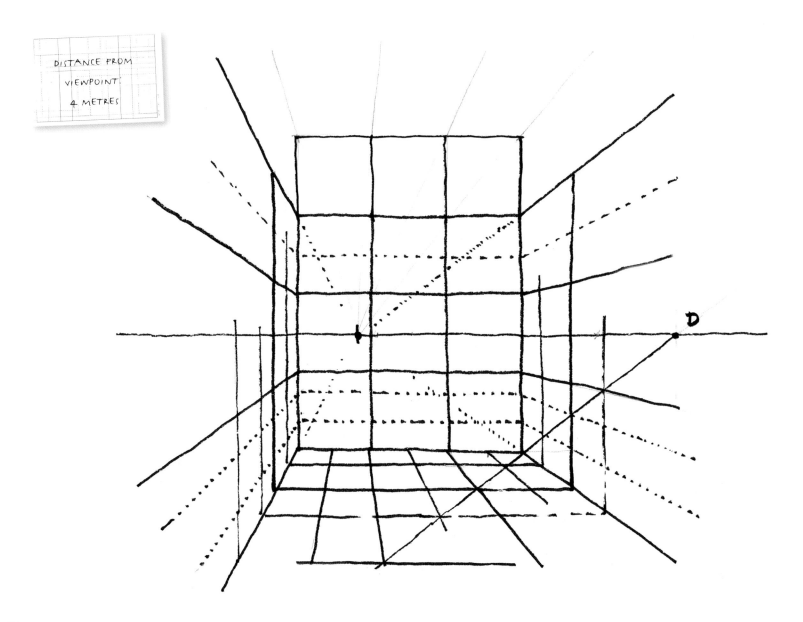

DISTANCE FROM
VIEWPOINT
4 METRES

D

This grid shows a larger room, but note that the width is not restrictive – you can make it the width you want, in which case the sides are drawn starting from the vanishing lines on the floor.

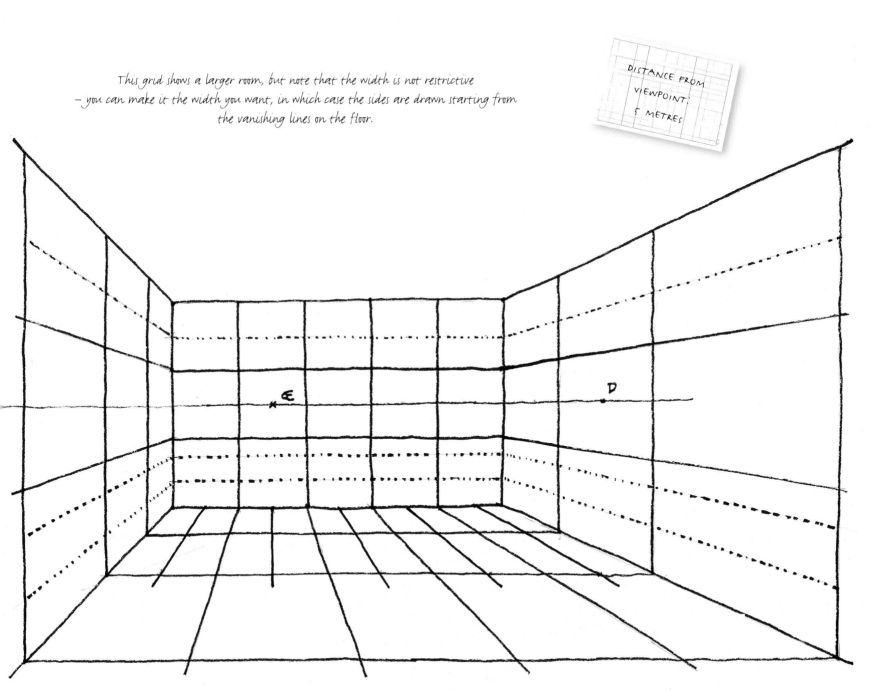

DISTANCE FROM VIEWPOINT: 5 METRES

Grids for oblique views

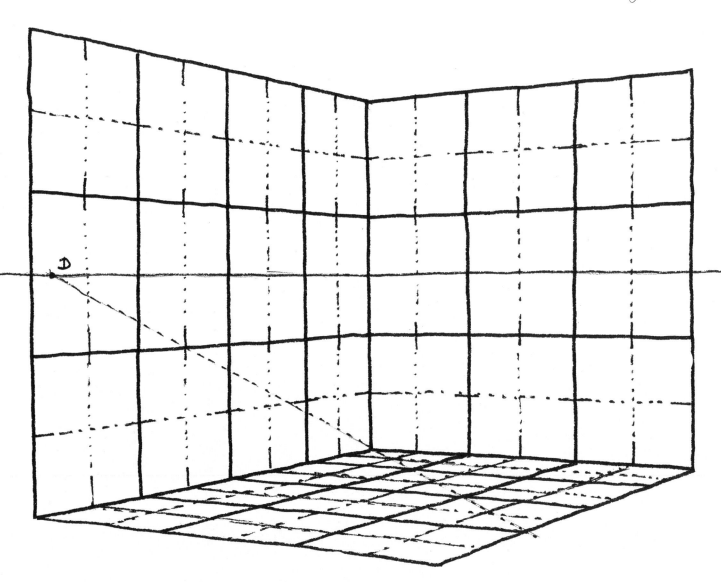

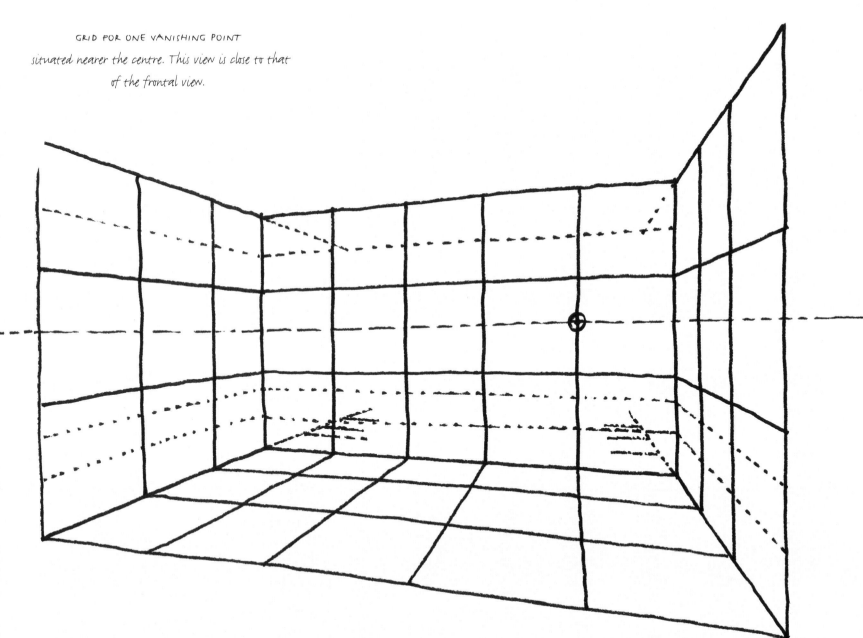

GRID FOR ONE VANISHING POINT
situated nearer the centre. This view is close to that
of the frontal view.

87